Freedom from Fatigue

Tammy Guest

Yellow Rose Publishing Ltd

First published in the United Kingdom in 2016 by

Yellow Rose Publishing Ltd

Copyright © Tammy Guest 2016

The right of Tammy Guest to be identified as the Author of the Work.

A CIP catalogue record for this title is available from the British Library

ISBN 978-0-9574098-3-5

Printed and bound by Lightening Source UK Ltd

Disclaimer

I have tried to recreate events, locales and conversations from my memories of them. In order to maintain their anonymity in some instances I have changed the names of individuals and may have changed some identifying characteristics.

Dedicated to:

My gorgeous husband, Murray Guest.

Who has loved me through the ups, downs, ins and outs of my journey with adrenal fatigue. Who has also been there as a sounding board for my entrepreneurial journey and continues to be my touchstone.

Acknowledgments

My Mum and Dad, for having me and raising me to be an individual.

My kids Mia, Noah and Elliot for inspiring me to be the best I can be as a Mum and female role model.

My sister Melita for putting up with an A type go getter as a big sister and never judging me.

My gorgeous publisher Nicola for keeping me on track to get such an important message out there.

Belinda for her support and her way with words.

To all the people who have ever worked with me, I appreciate your patience and faith.

The incredible Naomi and our connection on our walk and talks and time at the farm.

My amazing, female entrepreneurial friends and clients for allowing me to live my passion.

Preface / Prologue

This is a book for all the mums and businesswomen who need a lift and re-direction back to themselves. Somewhere in the midst of all this striving to keep the house, be the best wife, the attentive mum, the dutiful daughter, and the successful businesswoman, we lost what it is to be ourselves.

This is a story of my dance with myself, my health, my business and my family, whilst sharing what I know from years of experience as a scientist and naturopath, helping thousands of women regain their spark.

This book isn't... a textbook, a dissertation, a thesis or any other variety of scientific journal article.

It is simply what I know has worked – not only for me but for the thousands of women I have helped. It is my wish that you are filled with a sense of not being alone, not feeling like you are going nuts, and knowing that there is hope and that it's in your hands.

Contents

Part I

Part II

Healing

Entrepreneurial

Adrenal Fatigue

PART I

What I learnt from a Petri Dish

My background is in cancer research. Actually, I should go further back than that. I have had a gamut of jobs, from teaching gymnastics, to chopping up people's bits for a living in a morgue, to cancer research, to pulling pints, to testing poo, wee, spit and semen, going into clinical practice as a naturopath and nutritionist and then creating and running businesses.

The commonality between all of these is my love and awe of the human body and the people who inhabit them.

During my time in cancer research, I learnt some amazing things. The main one that has stuck with me is how cells work best.

Given the right environment, our cells do exactly what they need to do to regain balance.
In the lab, if we wanted to grow cells to test chemo drugs, we would pop them in a petri dish and put just the right amount of growth medium on them. Growth medium is a fluid that contains just the right acidity, alkalinity, vitamins, minerals and hormones to grow human cells. We would then put that petri dish in a stable environment that it loved – like an incubator at 37 degrees Celsius with the right humidity. And the next morning, like magic, we would have a beautiful layer of cells to test, like a thin layer of skin.

Now, if we took those same cells in the Petri dish and changed one thing about the growth medium or fluid they sat in, and then kept pulling the lid on and off, and taking them in and out of an environment they didn't like, the next morning we would end up with infected cells, some overgrowing and forming tumor-like structures, and others dying.

What stuck with me is that our human form is a big bag of three trillion cells. Those cells sit within fluid in which we constantly change the vitamins, minerals, hormones and pH level, and we move this bag of three trillion cells in and out of environments it doesn't like very much – work we don't like, challenging relationships, and we spend so much time in those places every week.

Yet we are all befuddled when things in our bodies change?

In this book, we will be exploring the four steps that I have used with thousands of clients – and with myself – to move through adrenal fatigue.

We start by remembering who we are and remembering we have a body. This may seem a bit silly to some but it is so prevalent when we get swept up in the ambitious world of hustle, strive and drive, to forget about our bodies.

We then explore the removal of any obstacles to our optimal energy. We go through the practicalities of a detox and the ground work for great gut health as well as the hidden systems that could be holding you back – ones that your doctor has unlikely checked out. If you are into the 'Why' and the science, then this is the part for you.

The third step is re-defining your medicine. Medicine, as we know it, has only existed in its current format for a century or so, which in the span of humans over time is smaller than a blip. It's what we are trained to go to when we need healing, but there are so many things that can be therapeutic when it comes to the individual, so we'll get to play with what that is for you.

The final step is to recharge. Adrenally fatigued entrepreneurs know perfectly well how to recharge their phones and laptops but we rarely take notice of our own 'batteries.' In this part of the book, we look at what has worked for thousands of my clients.

Remembering you have a body

The morning I remembered I had a body was in an ambulance between two Portuguese hospitals in my early twenties. I had been living my life of backpacking freedom and fun. The day prior I had arrived in Lagos, a beautiful coastal town in Portugal, after having an amazing time travelling through Spain and France. That day was stunning, the sun on the ocean and the waterside bars ready with their two for one cocktails. I checked into my pension accommodation on the 6th floor of an apartment building just back from the main piazza and headed down to make the most of those drinks specials.

Back then I didn't know what I now know about the mind and body. My priorities were around having a great time, meeting like-minded people and usually being the life of the party by getting wasted. So that afternoon's two for one cocktails led to an impromptu pub crawl and a wonderfully flirtatious encounter with a Welshman I just met.

This took us, barefoot, to the break wall on the waterfront in the pitch black and I was keen to jump down to what I thought was the sandy beach. The 'sand' actually ended up being a jagged outcrop of granite and my feet – which I had completely taken for granted – ended up with five broken bones. Although I wasn't aware of this in my drunken state and proceeded to walk up twelve flights of stairs in an identical building to the one I was staying in, only to find the apartment building next door was my accommodation. The following morning my feet were as round as two soccer balls on the base, my head felt like it was exploding, my muscles ached and stiffened, I felt my skin stabbing from the scratches I had acquired somewhere the day before, and I wanted to vomit.

My body was screaming at me!

I felt every cell when I hobbled, with only a broomstick to lean on, to the taxi rank to get to the nearest health clinic. It was there that they transferred me via ambulance to the larger hospital.

No one but the radiologist spoke English, which made me even more acutely aware of my body's state as there was no way to dispel the pain by talking about it. Whilst I was sitting with him and he was explaining the three broken bones in my right foot, I was hiding my left foot because I was determined to continue my journey down to Morocco.

Just to make sure I was *really* hearing my body, after the tests and two plaster casts, I was spat out to the emergency department with no pain medication or crutches because I was a foreigner.
My determination to have the journey I wanted led me to completely disregard any messages my body was giving me, time and time again.

So often we wander around, ignoring that we have a body, those little niggling pains, levels of stress and symptoms that we take for granted because we've had them all along. What is your body putting up with?

It's time to take a little body scan...

It's a check-in that most of us don't usually take the time to do for our bodies. You simply make your way through all the different systems of your body and check in to see what's been going on with it.

What has happened to your body? What has it been through?

Anything you tick represents physical stressors and all of these things are going to impact on your adrenal health because your adrenal glands register not only body stress, but emotional stress, psychological stress and mental stress too. Checking in is really important to understand where you're at.

Take a few minutes to complete The Body Scan over the next few pages...

Are you currently experiencing or have you ever experienced any of the following?

The Body Scan

(Tick all that apply)

SKIN

Rashes	☐
Lumps	☐
Soreness	☐
Itchy	☐
Psoriasis	☐
Eczema	☐
Lesions	☐
Warts	☐
Breakout	☐

GASTROINTESTINAL

Heartburn	☐
Burping	☐
Nausea	☐
Appetite Increase / Decrease	☐
Diarrhoea	☐
Bloating	☐
Constipation	☐
Gas	☐

EAR, NOSE and THROAT

Earache	☐
Decreased hearing	☐
Tinnitus	☐
Discharge	☐
Hay fever	☐
Sinusitis	☐
Infection	☐
Tonsillitis	☐

URINARY

Night time urination	☐
Infection(s)	☐
Burning / Stinging	☐
Sensation of Urination	☐
Urgency	☐
Dribbling	☐
Pain	☐
Incomplete	☐

REPRODUCTIVE

Pain ☐
Premenstrual Tension ☐
Menopause ☐
Prostate Problems ☐
Breast Lumps ☐
Breast Tenderness ☐
Pregnant ☐

EYES

Pain ☐
Double Vision ☐
Redness ☐
Visual Disturbances ☐
Watery ☐
Itchy ☐

RESPIRATORY

Cough ☐
Mucus ☐
Wheezing ☐
Chest pain ☐

NEUROLOGICAL

Dizziness ☐
Faints ☐
Numbness ☐
Tingling ☐

CARDIAC

Hypertension ☐
Pain ☐
Cold Extremities ☐
Shortness of Breath ☐
Palpitations ☐

MUSCULOSKELETAL

Pain ☐
Limited Range ☐
Stiffness ☐
Achy ☐
Injury ☐

OTHER SYMPTOMS

Fatigue ☐
Depression ☐
Memory issues ☐
Insomnia ☐
Difficulty sleeping ☐
Panic attacks ☐
Anxiety ☐

HEAD

Headaches ☐
Injury ☐
Migraine ☐
Hair Loss ☐
Brain fog ☐

Now that you've completed your check-in, what did you notice?

Were you aware of those different things?

Have you checked in with your body recently and known that there is a difference?

Or, did you find a bit of a surprise as to how many ticks you had? Or perhaps it was a nice surprise that you didn't have a lot?

Was there anything new that you hadn't noticed before?

Often we notice that there's a weak spot in most people's bodies, a bit like if we've had an injury earlier in our lives – for instance, a netball player with recurrent knee problems. When we're rundown or tired, it's the place that usually goes first. For some people, it's recurrent upper respiratory tract infections or the common cold or flu. Or maybe their tummy always goes when they're a bit rundown. For others, it might be something else. Just have a look and see which one is your weak spot.

The interesting thing I have found for entrepreneurs is that this weak spot is usually triggered by an upper limit. Upper limiting is the term introduced by Gay Hendricks in his book, *The Big Leap*. It's used to describe moving from one level up to another whole way of being. Interestingly, this is the time I usually see entrepreneurs have issues with their health.

For me, it's the upper respiratory tract infection. I have a history of pneumonia and tonsillitis when I have been run down. When I first moved to London from Australia, ready to take on the world as this amazing individual exploring my freedom, I came down with pneumonia.

During my final exams for my naturopathy degree, about to take on the world and live my purpose, I had viral and bacterial tonsillitis. After I ran my first retreat, even though I hadn't had a day off in four years or taken antibiotics in five years, I came down with pneumonia. My upper limit in all these cases was discovering a new level of being.

I've found it's helpful to think about the body having its own sentience. Your body is different to your Self. Your Self is the part of you with dreams, visions and aspirations. Your body goes along for the ride.

Our body gives us signs and signals all day. It's not very good at speaking English – a bit like having a puppy dog, or a pet, or for those of you with kids, it's a bit like having an extra child. When we are children, our body gives us signals when we are hungry, tired or playful and we follow them. As adults it goes around all day, every day, dragging its feet, following you around. When it wants to play, or it wants to have a rest, or it wants a drink of water, we ignore it for the more 'important' tasks we think we need to do. We drag it around with us here, there and everywhere, sometimes forgetting to give it water, sometimes forgetting to feed it and often forgetting to play. If your body truly were a pet or child, wouldn't we consider that abuse?

So when you've looked at all of those ticks on your body scan, is there something that you need to focus on to help you feel well and more energised?

This simple and enlightening exercise is to invite you to focus a little more and be more present to what's actually happening within your body, so that we can focus on this in the coming chapters.

Remembering who you are

I didn't go to Bali to remember who I was, I thought I already knew.

Three weeks before I was flying out to Bali for a month-long Entrepreneurial Incubator, where I was going to learn how to make my business go global, I had a conversation with a great friend of mine. She is one of those friends that just asks the right questions to really have deep conversations.
Her questions for me that day included,

"Do you know who you are?" and,

"Why are you heading to Bali?"

I had been listening to versions of these same questions for weeks. Being a mum of three and running a very busy clinic, it was a little difficult for some people to understand.

My answer to her was,
"Of course I do, for me every trip has a purpose. We go away as a family once a year for quality experiences, we go away as a couple once per year to reconnect, I run my retreats, I go on a business trip, and this trip I'm determined to learn how to get my message to reach as many people as possible."

Ten days before my trip I received a phone call...

"Hi, I'm sorry to have to do this, but we don't have the numbers, so we are cancelling the program, would you like to reschedule?"

In my head I thought, 'What on earth? How can you do that? I've been preparing my clinic, my clients, my staff, my practitioner's, my family, my kids, my husband, my finances, my systems, my health, my life… to go to Bali for an entire month!
No I can't reschedule!'

But after I had taken a couple of big breaths and spoken to my husband, we came to the conclusion that I could still do all I intended in Bali, just without the program, and I had essentially given myself the time to do it.

The first few days in Bali was record breaking in the amount of work I got done. I hit the ground running and by day three I had pretty much done three months worth of work. And it was day three that I was introduced to the flow of Ecstatic Dance, the freedom of scooter riding to new places, meeting new people and setting up a session with a shamanic healer.

Through all these experiences, parts of me lit up. I experienced feelings in my body I hadn't felt for a while; exhilaration, exploration, adventure and connectedness.

The insightful session with the shamanic healer led me to a week-long women's circle exploring our relationship with the feminine, the divine, the masculine, the earth and ourselves. A wonderful contrast to my entrepreneurial scientist identity.

After the circle I went back to finish off my 'to do' list and was looking to update some of my videos. The woman looking back at me in those earlier videos screamed adrenal fatigue. Her laser eyes and focus hiding her fatigue and burnout. The single-minded determination to get her point across left no room for flow and ease.

There were so many obvious similarities with her and the thousands of women I treat for adrenal fatigue. She was *me* only a few months earlier, and I hadn't even noticed.

The experiences I was having felt as though they were taking away layers I hadn't even noticed I had accumulated. The thing is, I didn't go to Bali to remember who I was, as I thought I already knew.

I truly believe who we are can surprise us, if we just allow it.

But we can't all go to Bali to accidently remember who we are so the following exercises are set to start you on the process.

The globe model

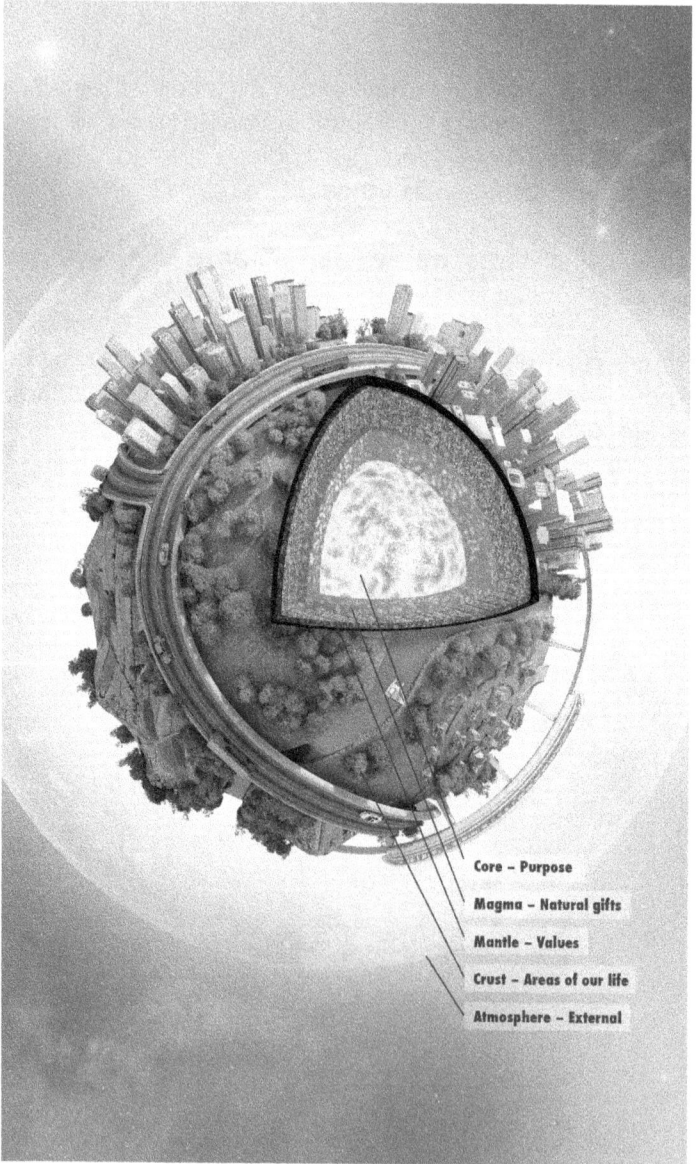

Core – Purpose
Magma – Natural gifts
Mantle – Values
Crust – Areas of our life
Atmosphere – External

You might be wondering why we are starting here, with you. I mean 'healing naturally from adrenal burnout' you might be thinking, well where's the things I need to take? Can't you just tell me the short cut?

The thing is, how we are in the world and how we heal or fix things can be similar to the globe of the world itself.

Let's just say we have our house or business on a fault line, an area prone to earthquakes. Of course we could just build again doing the same old thing and potentially get the same result, or we could look at what was happening underneath. The problem doesn't lie at the surface on the fault line, it started a lot deeper than that.

When we look at the model above, the molten core always remains molten, always fluid, it is unchanging. This is similar to our purpose. Why we were born in the first place and what we are here to do in this lifetime.

The next layer is the magma, this again is fluid but generally heads in directions of least resistance. This is a lot like our natural gifts, the things we are naturally talented at. Sometimes they are slow moving, sometimes they come out all of a sudden. Nurturing them allows for flow and ease. Bottle them up and don't let them out and we end up with a big explosion.
The mantle layer is the values, it is our basis on building foundations of our lives. There is an exercise below for more insights into your values.

The crust is similar to the continents we have on earth and represent the different areas of your life. Some might be business, family, relationships, finances, career, and creativity. Sometimes these 'continents' rub up against each other causing friction. Some area's are better built up and looked after than others but we also know that the wellbeing of the entire globe is dependent on the wellbeing of the whole, not just a focus in one area.

The final layer is the atmosphere, this is the environment, energy and information sphere we are surrounded by. We are both influenced by and influencing this. For you it could be society, the internet, media, and other people's energy.

You can see if we just tried to heal from the outside it's a lot of work for a small amount of reward and it will only work for a short period of time, it might look nice to others but the foundations are rocky. Whereas if we go back to the core and work our way out, then we have alignment.

Finding your values

Values are a way of recognising some of the choices that we make and how we make them. And maybe some of the hiccups we've had in the past with wondering why we choose some things and to do them so easily, yet others seem so hard to stick to.

As Dr John Demartini says, it all comes down to what you value. Now, a lot of us believe we value things like family, money, and maybe we even think we value our health. But the easiest way to see what we really value is to look around you.

I invite you to now to turn the page and complete the questionnaire about your surroundings.

Assessment of your surroundings

Answer the following questions honestly, be true to yourself...

Home

If I came to your house, what would I see?

Your environment. But what would I see in the colours that I saw?

Would it be white, stark and clinical? Or are there warm, earthy tones?

Is there vibrancy?

Is there clutter or is there space?

Are there family or pet photos on the wall?

Are there pieces of memorabilia from traveling, art, books, technology?

Health

If I came into your kitchen what foods would I find?

Would I find healthy fruit and vegetables or ready-made meals?

Do you take daily exercise, if so, what do you love the most?

Office

If I went to your office, what would I find?

What would I find in your inbox?

What are the things you subscribe to?

What are the pages that you like on Facebook, Instagram, Pinterest?

Finance

What do you spend your money on when you've got that last $5.00 or that last $20.00 note?

What is it that you prioritise to spend money on and what could you not live without?

What's that thing that you must have?

Your appearance

What would I see if I looked at your clothes?

Would they be a particular style, like sporty, fluid or business like?

What are the particular colours that you wear?

Your thoughts

What do you spend your time on?

What do you think about during the day?

What do you find yourself daydreaming about; holidays, a new car, seeing your friends or is it spending time doing a particular activity?

Where do your conversations turn to?

When you end up having those conversations, those big, deep, meaningful conversations or even the gossipy kinds of conversations, what's the topic that you always end up turning to?

With all this fresh in your mind, I invite you to write a list of your core values. *(What words, phrases, themes appear most frequently?)*

Now, I'd like you to check out what the themes are. These are the things that you value. You'll notice that there's generally a common thread and this is how you prioritise what you spend your time and money on, this is how you make your choices.

You may notice that healthy food, or health, or maybe even yourself in general, may not appear high on your list. This is why many of the things that you've done in the past might not have stuck when it's come to your health. Having an awareness is the best way forward. From awareness you can then make an informed choice and have the option to choose something different.

Your version of happy and healthy

The majority of clients I see answer 'Happy and Healthy' to their desired outcome from their visit at my clinic. But what I've found over my years of practice and my internal searching is that everyone's definition of happy is different. Until we have clarity on what that is for you then it is hard to know what to aim for.

Until I did this exercise, I thought everybody wanted to be happy and healthy like I did, that they wanted agility, freedom, adventure, and ease. But I found that we're all different and that we've all been defined by our past experiences, our likes, our dislikes, our preferences, our home and social situation, our genetics, our epigenetics, and the list goes on.

I found after doing this in a retreat group that some people really want security, safety, simplicity and slowness, which is entirely different to how I defined happy and healthy personally. What's your definition of happy and healthy? I'm going to help you find out what it looks like for you.

The following exercise will take about 15 minutes and it would be best during a quiet, uninterrupted time. It's not an exercise you need to overthink; the first thing that comes to mind is usually the thing you need to think about. Don't worry where the thoughts come from, just go with the process and see what comes up for you.

Find a comfortable spot and think about a time in your life, probably during primary school, when you were happy, when you felt the most YOU that you've ever felt.

Where were you, was it at school, home or somewhere else?

Who was you with, was it your family, friends or were you alone?

What does that happiness look like?
Don't over think this; it doesn't have to be complicated. Whatever comes for you is the right thing for you to be focusing on right now.

How did you feel at that time when you were the most YOU?

You know those feelings when you were YOU and not anyone else? You were just you in your uniqueness, like nobody else, and you loved it, and you were really happy.

Think about all of those different aspects about where you were, who was there, what was it like. But really think about how you felt and try to describe it, something other than 'happy'. Be more specific and go into detail about your actual feelings.

I'm sure you can feel that feeling right now.

Remembering that feeling, now I want you to think about a time during high school when you were at your happiest.

There's usually a standout moment for everybody every seven years of their life. Think about that time when you were most happy, when you were the most YOU have been. But if you find it difficult in your teenage years, then jump to your early twenties, and allow that moment to appear in your mind.

Where were you this time?

What were you doing?

Who were you with?

What was it like?

Okay, don't lose that feeling. Hold onto it and imagine it as a ball of light that you can take anywhere you go. This is your power and your uniqueness. Wherever or whatever makes you feel this inside, that's the thing you should do. If you're asked a question or given a choice, you should follow that feeling for the answer.

Write down the moments that you remembered, especially how it made you feel and the emotions. Try to get as specific as you can. Happy is generic, try feelings like ecstatic, warm, or cozy, content, or orgasmic.

Describe how it makes you feel in detail?

Now I'd like you to go and check out a thesaurus as well. Chose 5 of the best feelings for you then use your thesaurus to find other words to describe those exact same feelings.

1.

2.

3.

4.

5.

The art of manifestation

I'm sure everybody's heard of the book, *The Secret* and, if you haven't, it's a good book and movie to check out. *The Secret* is a documentary that is based around the idea or philosophy that you can create whatever you want in your life through thinking about it and making it become real – therefore manifesting it.

I love this idea and I have done a lot research to find out about how that actually happens, how the science of it really occurs.

When it comes to manifestation, there is the art side of it. This is the creative part where you come up with the things that you would like in your life. Some of these are really easy, like the time I wanted to upgrade my car to a Honda CRV, I want to own a new microscope, I want to climb Machu Picchu in Peru, I want to travel to see the Taj Mahal. As soon as you say those words, the majority of us can see it in our mind's eye. There's an art to doing that.

The other side to manifesting is the science. The science behind it all comes down to the way your brain works and the main part of this is pattern recognition.

Basically, what happens when you manifest something into your life is that you first have to think up what you would like and set an intention, and then you have to create action to register that with your mind and body. Sitting around just thinking about it going, *yes, I wish I had such and such* then not actually taking any action on it, isn't going to create the response that you want.

You have to think about it, visualise it, feel it, believe it will happen and then take action and step towards it.

What our brain is designed to do is answer questions and recognise patterns. If I was to say to you one plus one and then I continued talking, you'd still wonder when I was going to get back to the number two. Or, if I said purple cow and you try to think of anything but the purple cow, it becomes very difficult because your brain is set up to find patterns, and to visualise to answer questions.

One of the easiest ways to use this to your advantage is to create a vision board. A vision board is a series of pictures and we use this tool because our brain actually work in a visual format. You'll notice this when you're having a dream. It's not like it spells it all out for you in the written language, it's in pictures and symbols too. This is why most signs and instructions have symbols on them. There's a quick pattern recognition for our brain to deal with and receive the information that it requires. What we need to be doing when it comes to creating something in our lives, is to create the feeling of having it already, craft the experiences we want and create that pattern in our lives for our brains to recognise them.

One of the ways that we can do that is through visualisation. Creating a vision board, for anyone who hasn't done it before, is gathering pictures and images and phrases that invoke the feeling or the emotion or give us a clear picture of the things we actually want. Once we've done that, our brains see those images in our mind's eye and then attempts to match that in our life. Our subconscious now has a clear picture of the things that it's trying to match.

Some people might have noticed this pattern recognition

through having an injury or an ailment like having a broken leg. If you've ever had a broken leg or a broken arm or if you've ever had to be in a wheelchair, it's incredible how much you notice handicap lanes. It's amazing how much you notice steps. It's extraordinary how much you notice everybody else who has a broken leg, or a broken arm, or others in a wheelchair. The same thing happens with pregnancy. When people know that they're pregnant or think that they might be, everything comes on the television that has to do with a baby. Everything comes into your life that has to do with pregnancy or having a child. It's not something weird or out of the ordinary. Our brain is hardwired to recognise a pattern. Our subconscious has found something that is important to us at that time and it tries to seek things to match it with.

The exact same thing happens when you create a vision board. You set up those pictures. You look at them in the morning and at night before you go to bed. Then, during the next day, your brain will be hardwired to try and find things that will get you closer to those pictures.

How to create a vision board

1. Get a board - large cardboard or a pin board works best.
2. Collect your inspiration; for this you will need photos, magazines, newspapers, Pinterest or the Internet.
3. Cut out any images or words that stand out to you that you want to bring into your life. If you are on the computer you could print these out or pop them on a Pinterest page.
4. Add the final touches, you may want to colour the background, add glitter, sparkle or write your own affirmations or quotes.
5. Place your board somewhere you will see it daily.

The next step is visualisation – an absolutely incredible tool. Visualisation or seeing in your mind's eye, the outcome to an event before it happens has been long known in the elite sporting community as a psychological tool to enhance performance outcomes.

A simple Google search turns up 1.27 million results for 'Visualisation in Sport'. It is said that a well known Manchester United striker asks for the details of the colours of the opposing team, and their own uniform the night before a big game, to have a very clear image in his head of the way he would like to see the game end as well as the perfect kick of the ball. Visualisation has been used by other greats like Muhammad Ali, Michael Phelps and Tiger Woods to not only get the best out of their bodies but the best out of themselves.

Our missing link to get all we dream and desire in our life is to visualise. Have a very clear picture of that goal and get that dream and that feeling – in our mind even before any of it is going to occur.

Visualising how you'd like your life to be, visualising how you would like to feel and look for you. If you do that for five minutes every day, even for as little as a month, and you have a very clear vision of it, then research suggests you're going to get closer to that goal. I find it absolutely fascinating and incredible.

On a personal note, a few years ago I signed up with a coach. If you haven't come across a coach before, there are life coaches, business coaches, health coaches – a coach for anything really. These are people who have your back and can employ different means and strategies to get you to your goal. So, a couple of years ago, my coach did a guided visualisation with me. She talked me through a visualisation where all I had to do was get into a calm state, sit and think about where I wanted to be. So I visualised where I wanted to be twelve months from that time.

I visualised myself at that point in time meeting and introducing myself to the 'new' me twelve months in the future, explaining what was happening for me. At that time, I envisioned going to the front of a beautiful, very clean-looking shop front, with a clear glass door. I walked in and noticed how I looked in the future. I was very, very happy. I walked down a long corridor, got to the back room; it was a funny-shaped room and I kept my focus.

It had a little door at the back and my desk was there. I spoke to myself, and visualised everything that was in the room. Then I walked back out noticing different things along the way, like a beautiful waiting area, a lovely desk at the front. I looked at my future self admiring my long hair, and some very nice red boots on my feet. I thanked my future me and walked out the door. That was a lovely daydream, I thought.

Three weeks later my lease came up on the building that I was working from at the time, which was on the third floor of a pretty much abandoned building near a methadone clinic.

I thought, '*oh, this is interesting. I wonder if this twelve month time thing really exists*?'

Less than three weeks later I was set-up in my new, beautiful clinic which is exactly what I had visualised during the meditation with my coach. The same clear doorway, the strange shaped office and even the exact red boots! It was even better than I expected and I truly was very, very happy. I had a gorgeous place to fulfill my dream of helping my local community with their health. To have a shop front to invite clients in, where they felt safe and looked after.

Now I can't describe how this actually happened, because, of all the places that could've become available, this one did. Of all the places that were going to have the layout of the one in my visualisation, this one did. I didn't even know these premises existed. So, the power of visualisation manifestation goes beyond the subconscious level.

But, as far as my science goes, it's pattern recognition where the mind tries to find the best match to your visualisation or the thing that you've set an intention for.

The final step is action. The last thing that you need to do when it comes to manifestation is not just sit there and say to yourself, '*Okay, I want to lose weight. I want to lose weight. I want to lose weight.*'

To lose weight, you need to first stick an image of what releasing your weight looks like to you on your vision board. What your future you looks like, it might be an old picture where you were happy and healthy or one you find in a magazine. Like my friend Denise Duffield-Thomas of *Lucky Bitch* says, "That's not going to work if you don't get off your couch is it?"

So, the final action step that you need to take is whatever needs to be done to get you closer to the picture in your head, that picture on your vision board.

Taking an action step is going to set you up to succeed. It might be making a phone call to find out who can help you along the way, or what class you need to join, or finish reading this book and implementing all that you have learnt.

Any of those action steps creates yet pattern recognition for your brain that you're actually doing something towards it and you want more of that. Your brain can then find more patterns to recognise.

One of my favourite action steps for manifesting things into my life, which I learnt from Denise, is to change all of your passwords to whatever it is that you want to create. For some people, it might be their level of health, their body or their dream holiday destination, and the date. The date is a very important thing. Having a date on there is going to ensure that your mind is ready and set for that date rather than just leaving it open – if it's open it could happen anytime in the future really.

So, your password could be a place that you want to go on holiday. It could be a magical number of lives you want to affect. It could be the make and model of the new car you would like. It could be the item or size of clothing that you'd love or the level of energy you want. It could be absolutely anything you'd like. So having that as your password for everything is an instant recognition for your mind every time you login to something.

The last little action that I like to take is to send myself reminders as though the thing has already happened. I have little reminders on my phone notifying me of my goals throughout the day. At one point in time it was,

'I have a thousand Likes on Facebook.'

This stemmed from my intention for everybody to know how to be inspired by their health. My thought process was that if I had a thousand Likes on Facebook, a thousand people are going to be inspired by their health.

So, on my phone I set up little messages to say,

'Congratulations, you've reached a thousand Likes.'

'Congratulations, a thousand people are interested in changing their health for the better.'

'Congratulations you've changed a thousand lives.'

All of those messages were popping up throughout my day. I might have been in the middle of something and all of a sudden I get this little reminder. Again, that pattern recognition occurs. Then all of a sudden, within a couple of weeks I had a thousand Likes on Facebook. It's incredible and I highly suggest you give it a go.

The other thing to remember with visualisation is that we all learn differently. One learning model suggests that the majority of us, which is about 40%, learn in a visual manner. We learn through our eyes and what we see, and we can see things in our mind's eye too.

Up to 30% use auditory learning styles. If this is you, it may be easier to make changes in your life if you to listen to things. For you, it might be leaving little voice-recorded messages on your phone or it might be recording your goals and then re-listening to them over and over again. Or it may be stimulating motivation by listening to podcasts or audiobooks.

The last learning style is kinesthetic. This is actually experiencing what it's going to be like. If you're a kinesthetic learner and you want to practice yoga, one of the best things you can do is to take an introductory class at a yoga studio that you like so that your body and your mind receive the pattern recognition of actually experiencing the feeling of yoga. If your goal is to have more creativity for less stress in your life then going to a drawing class would be ideal.

So make sure to incorporate your own learning style. Using these suggestions will have an impact on the way that your brain recognises the patterns that you want to feel, you want to see, and you want to hear around you.

As a side note, positive anticipation of your goals and gratitude are two of the most powerful tools to help your adrenal glands. There are a number of studies showing cortisol being affected by the ability to have something to look forward to, as well as creating moments of gratitude for the present and the past.

PART II

Remove all obstacles

In this next part of the book I get really practical on the 'how to' of removing obstacles for your health and vitality. I also give you all the science and why it works, but I found personally that it's not until we get curious and get out of our own way that the real wellbeing can shine through.

After being so health conscious all my life and finding the man of my dreams to start a family, it came as a shock to me that one of the biggest obstacles I had to hurdle in my life was falling pregnant. Everything else in my life that seemed difficult I could either think my way out of or work hard for and it just happened. School came pretty easily to me and I was top of the class. I loved getting the answers right and coming first. I have a folder filled with certificates from academic competitions that made me feel proud. The job I wanted as a kid was to be Australia's first female fighter pilot. I joined the Air Training Corps as a thirteen year old so that every chance I had I was flying in gliders, and fixed wing planes as a teenager, well before I was learning to drive a car.

So, when I wanted to create a whole new family member with my husband, after already completing a biomedical science degree and in my final year of my naturopathy degree, I was doing everything I scientifically knew to fall pregnant. I had the tick boxes in my head of what it would take – I had done a detox, I tested my hormones, I knew my cycle inside and out, I knew when I was most fertile, I was eating exactly the amount of macronutrients, I was supplementing with vitamins, herbs and shakes, I had taken my exercise down to 75%, I was even ticking the box of nesting by helping at the school of my husband's children.

It came as a shock to me that, after six months of trying, it hadn't happened. What I wasn't registering was how I might be standing in my own way and just how tired my body actually was.

The part I left out was that the year I was trying to fall pregnant was my final clinic year of naturopathy, I had more exams than my entire university career, and in addition I had a part-time job, on-call as a scientist at a hospital near the university. I got married in the April of that year, only to return to university which was interstate to my husband and step-kids.

This meant that every Thursday after university and work I would drive forty five minutes to the airport and fly home to spend the weekend with my family, help in the school canteen on a Monday morning then fly back interstate for my shift at the hospital in the afternoon. I'd go to Uni and work until Thursday when I would do this all over again. I was so busy being busy that I didn't realise how tired my body was.

Yes I was *doing* all the right things but who I was *being* through the process was holding me back. It's like having a checklist and ticking off the actions for the sake of ticking off the actions, and completing them being frustrated and mindlessly finishing them. Or you could be ticking them from a place inside yourself of contentment and ease, happy in the knowledge that you are heading toward your goal with appreciation and love.

Who you are *being* in any given moment creates chemicals in your body and they in turn affect your other systems.

When I had handed in my resignation and the weight and stress of the running around had eased. I settled in with my husband and kids, surrounded by love and fun, over the final Uni holidays, I discovered I was pregnant.

Hindsight is an incredible thing and you might be thinking it's fairly obvious that my adrenals might have been pushed to the limit, but when I was in it, focused on my goal, I really didn't see it. This is the case for so many of my clients and it might be the case for you too. Exercising daily without a day off, crossfit, training for marathons, climbing mountains or corporate ladders are all unseen obstacles standing in the way of vibrant, vital wellbeing.

There is an old wives tale that has some scientific validity. If you have a pot of boiling water and drop a frog in, it will instantly jump out or die. If you have a frog in cold water and it incrementally increases to boiling, the frog doesn't notice that it is in fact, boiling water, and causes it so much harm that leads to its death.

So many of us are slowly killing ourselves, incrementally increasing our stress levels and putting ourselves in 'boiling water'. Saying yes to new clients, more work, more business, family commitments and not taking the time to check if we are actually doing ourselves damage.

Adrenal burnout – the science…

The science behind it, for those of you who are asking 'but how?'

Cortisol (hydrocortisone) is a glucocorticoid or steroid hormone produced by the adrenal gland. Cortisol increases blood sugar through a fancy chemical reaction called gluconeogenesis, it acts as a natural anti-inflammatory to suppress the immune system and helps in fat, protein and carbohydrate metabolism and decreases bone formation. Cortisol can literally burnout and become depleted in chronic inflammation and in adrenal fatigue.

The adrenal glands secrete lots of hormones but its two main ones are adrenalin and noradrenalin. These two hormones are released in response to stressful situations. Adrenalin is the reason for the "fight-or-flight" response to stress. Originally, adrenalin helped us escape the Saber-Tooth Tigers but nowadays, adrenalin is produced as a result of day to day modern stressors like being busy, phone calls, social media, fast food and too much coffee or wine.

When used properly adrenalin and noradrenalin will:

- Increase your heart rate and the heart pumping which increases blood pressure
- Move blood to the essential organs and away from your skin
- Increase blood sugar levels, so you can run faster from the 'Saber-Tooth Tiger!'
- Increase Metabolism
- Make you breathe faster and harder
- Dilate pupils
- Can make your hair stand on end
- And finally helps the blood thicken

Adrenal burnout, also known as adrenal fatigue or exhaustion happens in response to long-term physical and emotional stress. As certain vitamins and minerals are precursors to adrenalin and cortisol, if your food intake of these nutrients is too low, after an extended period, the body can no longer make enough cortisol and adrenalin. Adrenal burnout, scientifically, describes the adrenal glands lack of response to the brain's call for more hormones.

There are three stages of adrenal burnout;

Stage 1

The first stage's fancy name is hyper-adrenalism, and often has high cortisol levels and low DHEA levels. These tests are usually measured by saliva and your integrative health practitioner can order these for you.

Symptoms of high cortisol include insomnia, sugar cravings, confusion, weight gain, hot flushes and water retention. Cortisol also decreases your happy hormone levels which may lead to depression and insomnia.

Cortisol also messes with your immune system resulting with recurrent infections, long term inflammatory conditions and autoimmune disease.

High cortisol also can stop your thyroid hormone from converting to its active form. This can create a thyroid hormone imbalance and can play havoc on your metabolism.

Stage 2

During stage two, the hormone DHEA stays low but cortisol supplies will head in the low-normal range leaving you feeling tired and stressed, but functional.

Stage 3

It's during stage 3 where cortisol flat lines during the day and it becomes difficult to perform the most simple of functions.

Over the next section we will explore things you may have adjusted to that are actually standing in the way of your energy and goals.

But first let's flip the page to check on the Burnout warning signs...

Burnout Warning Signs

(If you answer 'Yes most of the time' to 5 or more below, you may be experiencing Adrenal Burnout)

Are you getting tired more easily?

Do you feel tired more than energetic?

Do you feel like you are working harder to get things done?

Are you experiencing more 'flat' days than usual?

Are you becoming more forgetful?

Are small things irritating you more than usual?

Are you seeing family and friends less frequently?

Are you too busy for routine things?

Are you exhausted in the mornings?

Is there a lull in your energy around 2 to 4pm in the afternoon?

Is your immune system having a hard time shaking things off?

Does sex seem like a chore?

Do you feel you've lost your spark?

Do you want to talk to people less?

Symptom cup

To remove obstacles in our way to perfect health, we need to firstly start with our symptoms so we're aware of what is going on in our body. Symptoms don't just appear from anywhere, they are usually the tip of an iceberg that has been building and building, a lot like a cup filling up and up and we don't notice until it spills over the top.

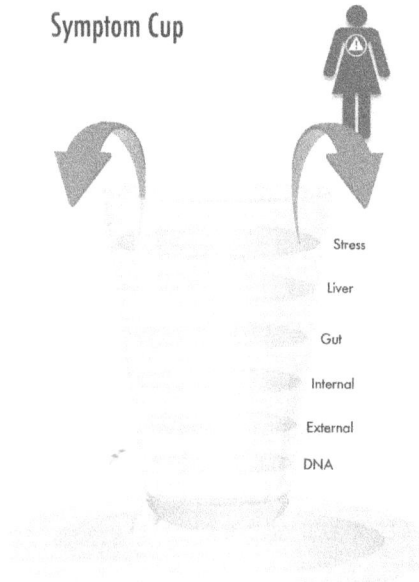

Symptom Cup

Stress

Liver

Gut

Internal

External

DNA

As you can see in the base of everyone's cup we all have some type of genetic influence. Your parents or someone in your family may have had something similar to you. Unlike you may have been taught, these aren't stand-alone symptoms. Psoriasis, although on the skin, has a very, very similar mechanism of action in your body as hay fever and migraines do. Any of these immune responses have a different manifestation in each person and generation.

Although they may each have the gene, some can be turned on and others can be turned off. Genes can be compared to a light switch – it can be switched on or off. When lined up with all the other genes (or light switches) it can manifest in various ways, such as psoriasis, eczema, hay fever, migraines and irritable bowel-like (IBS) conditions. In common, they each have a surface that's affected, with blood flow and the immune system underneath. They also have a trigger and they all need to be dealt with by the body to clear them so they don't keep reacting.

The next thing affecting the cup is your external environment. These are the things that you are responding to or reacting to externally.

This could be cleaning products, your makeup, certain grasses, pollens or pet even hair. Your body recognises that these substances aren't part of you and creates an immune response to them. That response can again accumulate over a 72-hour period and, on the flip side, can be taken away from your body and processed over about 72 hours as well.

The next contribution to your symptom cup is your internal environment which is anything you're ingesting. These are things like allergens or intolerances that you might be having only a small response to. For instance, the top five, when it comes to food intolerances in Australia at the time of printing, is gluten, whole wheat, lactose, cow's milk and soy. These immune responses to intolerances are measured by a protein called IgG that could be happening in your body. One of the reasons we have the amount of intolerances we currently have in western countries is because of overstimulation. We're used to having things like cereal or toast for breakfast, sandwiches for lunch, and pasta for dinner. Our bodies are in overload.

Unfortunately your body's response every single time you're exposed to the allergen is going to be more, and more, and more, and you're not going to give yourself that 72 hours to breakdown that immune complex that's formed.

The next stage is about your gastrointestinal lining or your mucous membrane integrity. So, all of the things that we just talked about with the external and internal environment have to enter our body somehow. This could be breathed in up your nose and into your sinuses, swallowed down to your gastrointestinal lining and into your mucous membrane, or even to your girly bits and boy bits. This is totally normal and a process your body can handle when it's in balance. The integrity of that surface and whether or not it can create a barrier is one of the most important things as to whether or not you're going to react to it.

The next layer of the symptom cup is all about your liver. Your liver, and how it functions, is one of the most important ways of getting those toxins and immune complexes out of your body in a timely fashion.

The last one, right on top of that cup, is stress. Stress will change everything. Your body's response to cortisol and adrenalin will have an incredible effect on the majority of those symptoms. As I mentioned earlier, stress uses up a whole bunch of nutrients that are really important for every other chemical reaction in that happens in the symptom cup.

If we look at the model of the cup again, and on a stressful day it is already half full, there is not a lot of room for other symptoms. Unfortunately those systems of the body also depend on the limited nutrients that stress is taking up, so the symptoms start to fill the cup to the brim. It's on these days that it doesn't take much for the symptom cup to run over into headaches, gut issues, sinus, hay fever, or skin flare ups.

As you can see, the health and wellbeing of each layer is going to make a difference on how your body either flows out into your symptomology or is minimised to not run over into psoriasis, eczema, hay fever, asthma, migraines or IBS. Your body does not know the difference between a physical stress or a psychological stress, it will have the same response either way. Each of the layers of the symptom cup are a physical stress that may become an obstacle to you have the abundance of energy you dream of, so ensuring their optimal wellness is a priority.

Weight loss and wellness

I used to be a gymnast. I trained hard and competed at a State level. When I stopped training and became a gymnastics coach, my body changed. My entire gymnastics career I had been flat chested; I was teased about it. But when I stopped, my chest grew, my tummy got wider, my hips, bottom and thighs all grew and I started to develop a more feminine shape.

The predominant model at the time was:

Energy In = Energy Out

The way I understood it, I was training less, so I needed to eat less. My closest friend at the time was on a diet and also bulimic; she seemed to be keeping her weight down, so I thought I could too. Apart from it being incredibly bad for your body, ripping apart your gut lining, changing your absorption, immunity and neurotransmitters; I couldn't stand the idea of vomiting so I just limited my food intake. Which in itself is literally starving your body of essential nutrients but at the time I didn't realise this. The same control and dedication I had in training, I refocused on food, or lack of it. The only meal I couldn't get away with was dinner so I ate that one meal a day with my family.

My body continued to grow and change, while my brain became foggier and I started to have dizzy spells. Luckily, my need to be good at school outweighed my need to be thin and I started to eat more again knowing my brain function, mood, metabolism and life depended on it. If I had continued to starve myself the ramifications on my hormones, digestion and mental health could have been far reaching and self destructive.

My story isn't dissimilar to so many women I have seen who have only been exposed to a completely outdated model of what healthy weight balance actually looks like… and it is doing us all damage.

The wellness wheel

The general consensus when it comes to the old-school way of thinking about weight loss, is it's based on energy in and energy out. Hopefully, if you've got that nice and balanced, you will be turning over your metabolism at a sufficient rate. If, for instance, you're sitting around not doing much, your metabolism isn't going to work. The weight loss isn't going to follow.

Unfortunately this is a pretty outdated model. It's all good and well to think about your energy in being your food and your energy out being your exercise and movement. But there are other things happening underneath the surface of your body that will hamper your ability to lose weight, create more energy or speed up your metabolism.

Wellness Wheel

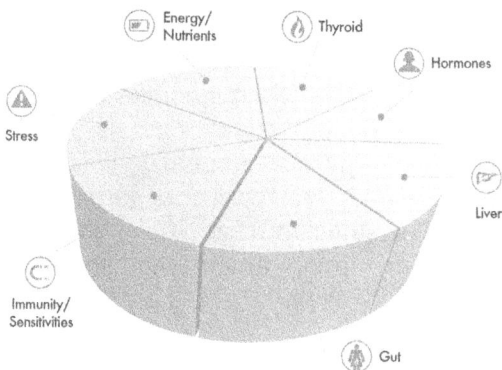

As you can see in the wellness wheel, we've got energy in and energy out. But it's only part of the pie. The next step, clockwise, is your Thyroid.

If your thyroid is doing a good job, it will be balancing your ability to increase and decrease your metabolism. But if your thyroid is really slow, then you'll be feeling colder than usual, you'll be sluggish and won't be metabolising very well. Your Thyroid stimulating hormone (TSH), when tested may appear higher than

2.0 and this can indicate a sluggish thyroid.

If you're experiencing any of these issues, you should see your health practitioner as they'll be hampering your ability to maintain a healthy weight and have all the energy you like.

The next segment of the wheel is your hormones. Hormones such as estrogen are considered toxins by your body and need to be detoxified through your liver. If not, it's stored in your fat cells – and for women, that's around your middle and your behind. Making sure that your liver pathway is working to get your estrogen out efficiently and keeping your hormones in balance is really important for maintaining a healthy weight, particularly around your middle.

Which brings us to the next segment, your liver, looking after your liver pathways and making sure that you're metabolising fats, toxins and hormones properly is going to be the best stepping stone to shifting weight and bringing your body into balance. Two of the best things you can do before embarking on a weight loss journey is to check your liver function and to do a good cleanse or detoxification to clear out those pathways.

Checking your liver function is traditionally done by a blood test called Liver Function Test (LFT), this test is used with parameters to let Doctors know if you need to be hospitalised or not. Functional Liver Detoxification Profile (FLDP) is a saliva and urine test that can be ordered by your integrative health practitioner through a functional medicine laboratory, giving you an indication of your optimal liver function.

The next part revolves around your gut. It's the first place that you're getting nutrients in. Those nutrients are going to be really important for getting that Weight Loss Wheel – and your metabolism – running effectively. You need to look after your gut lining so your gut bacteria is happy and your enzymes are working efficiently to absorb all the nutrients from your food.

Next in your Wellness Wheel is immunity and sensitivities. These can stop your metabolism because your body needs to spend so much more time looking after any immune complexes that are formed because of any infections or food intolerances you have. This means that your body spends a lot of time, effort and energy pulling those immune complexes apart and there isn't a lot of time, effort or energy left in your metabolism. Therefore actively avoiding your known intolerances is just another way to speed up your metabolism.

The last segment is stress. Most people are aware that stress can lead to weight gain or loss, and it's due to your stress hormones depleting vitamins and nutrients that are needed to fire up your metabolism. Combating stress with positive lifestyle choices can be a huge step towards your body letting go of fat.

By addressing all the different pieces of the wellness wheel, not just energy in and energy out, you will see your metabolism thrive.

Are you out of balance?

Let's check…

Answer the questions over the next few pages, if you answer yes to 2 or more in any section this could be hampering your ability to maintain a healthy weight and ample energy.

You don't need to answer yes to all of them to have an issue.

YOUR ENERGY

Do you move for 30 minutes a day 5 days a week?

THYROID

Do you feel the cold?

Do you sweat when everyone else seems cool?

Are your hair and nails brittle?

Do you 'hit a wall' at 9:30pm and have to go to sleep?

Find it difficult to shifting weight?

Do you feel sluggish?

LIVER

Do you have brain fog?

Can't concentrate?

Can't focus, especially in the afternoon?

Wake to urinate between 2 - 4am?

Have food sensitivities?

Any strange reactions to medications?

Do alcohol or caffeine affect you?

GUT

Loose stools?

Constipation?

History of antibiotic use or pain medication in the past 12 months?

Flatulence?

Burping?

Heartburn/reflux?

Bloating?

HORMONES

Pre menstrual tension?

Irregular periods?

Weight distribution changes to particularly around your middle / just below your belly button?

Hormonal headaches?

IMMUNITY

Glands swollen but don't seem to get sick?

Can't shake the cold or flu?

Multiple antibiotic use of the past 12 months?

FOOD SENSITIVITIES

Bloated after meals?

Feeling full when you've only eaten a little?

Gurgling or strange sounds from your tummy after eating certain foods?

Do some foods give you a 'food coma' or foggy head?

Itchy skin or blocked/runny nose after certain foods or beverages?

STRESS

Irritated by small things?

Too busy to perform routine tasks like answering your emails?

Don't feel like yourself or lost your spark?

Feeling sad or flat for no reason?

Sleep disturbances?

If you have answered yes to more than 2 in any section then this is the area you need to address to begin your journey to get your body back into balance.

The gut

Your gut is a twelve metre long tube that's just a big continuation of your skin. Just imagine your skin happens to turn a corner at your lips. It gets a little bit more complicated with some mucous layers, and it continues through your body until it hits the bottom where it turns a corner again and turns back into your skin that you see on the outside.

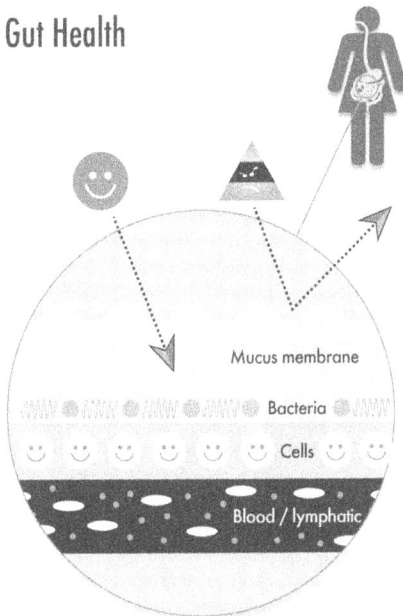

Gut Health

Mucus membrane

Bacteria

Cells

Blood / lymphatic

If we were to take that tube, pull it apart, cut it and look at it sideways like in the diagram, what you'd see is that the top layer is a mucous membrane – a squishy, clear substance very much like Aloe Vera. And like Aloe Vera, mucous is really dependent on water – another reason it is so important that you get enough water so that that the mucous membrane works properly.

Underneath that mucous lies a layer of bacteria. Probiotics (good bacteria) as well as bad bacteria and things like yeast all hang out there. Good bacteria and bad bacteria need a bit of a balance. I'm sure you've heard it before on the occasional TV advertisement. There needs to be a balance because the good bacteria have a range of jobs to do. We have the firemen who look after all the inflammation and heat in the gut; the policemen, looking after any brawls or any upsets that happen in your tummy; the nurses that look after all the little incidences that might arise; and there are some factory workers that just populate and fill up space – your general *Acidophilus* and *Bifidus* strains. But there are also other probiotic strains that have really specific jobs in the gut and in the body.

The bad bacteria, on the other hand, are havoc-makers, having brawls that you might see outside nightclubs, throwing their rubbish around, and bringing all their nasty friends in. Those hooligans can cause you long-term issues when it comes to food intolerances, allergens, IBS issues, as well as a lowered immune system and other autoimmune disorders.

There are three main things that are affected if you have an imbalance of good and bad bacteria.

1. The gut is the place where nutrients come in to be absorbed – we want this environment to be as welcoming as possible.

2. Your immune system – the gut is the first place that anything from your external environment comes in to. The issue here is, if you're starting to respond to things like bacteria, viruses or other pathogens like parasites, then your body needs to know about it. Those good and bad bacteria are the first response team to give that message to your body so it can create an immune response to the intruder.

3. Up to 75% of your neurotransmitters and their receptors are actually built in your gut lining. So, 75% of your happy hormones, your ability to feel happy, is built in your gut. Think about it. When you get that excited feeling – butterflies in your stomach, that's actually where your neurotransmitters are being built. If you can't optimally look after that gut lining then you're actually missing out on three quarters of your ability to feel happy. A quarter of it is left for your brain.

The next layer underneath the bacteria contain your cells. The strength of your cells and the integrity of those cell membranes is really important so any nasties don't get through. And underneath those cells is your blood.

To bring it all together, the nutrients from your food will soak all the way through the cell membranes and into your bloodstream, and head to exactly where they're needed in your body. Bad aspects of your food, including bacteria, viruses, allergies, intolerances or parasites, should slide off that mucous membrane, preventing those nasties from hitting your bloodstream.

Issues that happen within your gut lining – especially the mucous membrane integrity – are highly dependent on factors such as pH changes, stress, dehydration, if you've had anti-inflammatories, antihistamines, antibiotics, alcohol, antacids and other analgesics and pain medications.

It can take anywhere from 24 hours in the case of alcohol, up to 12 months in the case of some antibiotics to repair the damage done to the mucous membrane.

If that top layer, which is a lot like a force field, disappears, then those good bacteria that signed up for the wonderful jobs aren't really comfortable in that zone anymore. They signed up for a nice, cushy mattress and you've just taken it all away. So, they're out with the next poo. What happens then is that beautiful protective barrier that was looking after your gastrointestinal lining is also out with the next poo.

Unfortunately, all of those good things and all of those bad things that were sliding on past or soaking on in are now going to be hammering on a fairly raw lining, just the same as if you took the top layer of your skin off. It wouldn't really matter if you put the most beautiful, soft, cashmere sweater over the top of it, it would still be quite painful. You would feel the inflammation, the redness, the heat and the swelling just the same as what is happening in your gut lining.

That inflammation, heat and swelling unfortunately has nowhere to go in your gut lining and so it heads in between the cells. And because the cell integrity has been compromised, instead of tight junctions in between the cells, you have a permeable membrane or a 'leaky gut' as some people call it. Unfortunately, those things that were getting past before, like bacteria, viruses, allergens, intolerances and parasites, are now going to be leaking parts of themselves into your bloodstream. This is where your immune system starts to respond and you end up having even more allergies and intolerances. Often allergies or foods that you weren't even responding to before now become issues.

I can't emphasise enough how important it is to look after that gut lining. Things that we can do for the mucous membrane include looking after the mucous, keeping it nice and hydrated, plus ingesting adequate fibre and keeping those probiotics in.

Top ten tips to beat the bloat...

1. Avoid known food intolerances – gluten, dairy, wheat, corn, soy.
2. Minimise refined sugar- this feeds bad microbes in your tummy and ferments creating gas.
3. Check for parasites – if you have lived overseas, been brought up with animals or a rainwater tank, there is a chance you have a parasite. Complete digestive stool analysis CDSA or Faecal PCR can be completed by functional pathology laboratories to check for parasites.
4. Drink 2 litres of water a day.
5. Fibre is your friend – 1 tsp of Chia, LSA, or rice bran in some water daily will act like a scourer for your bowel.
6. Spices can decrease inflammation of the gut – add turmeric, cumin or fennel to foods.
7. Herbal teas for gut healing include Chamomile, Lemon Balm, Peppermint, Fennel, and Meadowsweet.
8. Mucilaginous foods – it's a fancy name for slippery foods to heal the mucous membrane include aloe vera juice, slippery elm or psyllium.
9. Fermented foods – try sauerkraut, kimchi, kefir, or kombucha. These foods contain good microbes that can aid your body's digestion, immunity, mental health and metabolism.
10. Probiotics – these are good microbes found naturally in fermented foods but can also be supplemented. They act like soldiers protecting the gut wall. Ask your integrative health practitioner which one is right for you.

Food intolerances

Most people think about foods and things that they might be reacting to as an instantaneous reaction. This rarely happens in your body unless you have a full-on Immunoglobulin E (IgE) mediated reaction, commonly known as an allergy.

Symptoms include hives or anaphylactic shock, resulting in a medical emergency. If we're talking about other symptoms like psoriasis, eczema, asthma, hay fever, migraines or IBS, these are all a cumulative kind of effect. These delayed responses are IgG or IgM that build up over time, generally around 72 hours. So you normally won't feel it immediately and the intolerance reactions can build on each other, a bit like filling a cup.

These reactions compound and you can overflow, resulting in the above symptoms. For example, if I have an intolerance to wheat and I have some toast in the morning, then a sandwich at lunch. I've filled up that symptom cup about a third of the way. Then the next day I have more toast for breakfast then pasta for lunch. I'm pushing it close to the top of that symptom cup. And then on the third day all of a sudden I get symptoms of brain fog, can't concentrate, fatigue, maybe headaches, sometimes skin conditions and often tummy types of reactions. You may just get one or multiple of these yourself. I've hit my overflow due to consistently consuming foods I am intolerant to.

As a side note, immune complexes that are formed when immunoglobulins (Ig) react are very much like a magnet and iron filings. Have you ever done that experiment where you place iron filings on a thin level surface and hover a magnet along the top? You'll remember the filings are picked up, which then forms a tight complex of magnet and iron filing. What happens in your body is that your immunoglobulins are very much like iron filings flittering around your body. When you eat food that you're intolerant to it's like sticking a big magnet in and forming that complex throughout your body.

Pulling apart magnets from iron filings is a really difficult thing. It takes quite some time, and your body can't handle that immune complex so it can't pull it apart easily. It does actually take about 72 hours for that to die down. To find out whether you're intolerant to particular foods, it's best to see your health professional as there are pathology tests that can do the job for you.

Gluten:

I often see clients with gluten-sensitivities in clinic and gluten sensitivity doesn't have to be celiac. It can be a different mechanism that creates a system where your body doesn't particularly respond well to gluten. Gluten tends to show up in behavioural disorders, issues with mood, with attention span, fatigue and a feeling of heaviness, some gastrointestinal complaints, as well as occasional skin conditions.

Dairy / Cow's Milk:

The next main trigger is cow's milk, or dairy. Back in caveman times, we only consumed *human* milk on a regular basis until about eighteen months old. So now, as adults, we're having issues with milk because we haven't developed the lactase enzymes to breakdown some of the proteins – not to mention the fact that we didn't consume the milk of another species. In my experience, dairy intolerance usually results in symptoms like sinusitis, hay fever style sneezes and recurrent ear infections – usually a variety of upper respiratory tract stuff. I highly suggest finding an alternative such as goat's milk, almond milk, rice milk, oat milk, coconut milk and in some cases, soy milk – although, soya can have both sensitivity issues in some individuals and hormone issues in others, so use sparingly.

Egg:

The last main trigger is egg. Although eggs are fantastic for us and a fantastic source of protein, if we consume them when we have a stressed out body, a poor gut and we're a bit fatigued, there is a chance that we may develop intolerance symptoms. Simply eliminate egg for 3 weeks and notice whether or not your body is actually reacting to it. Your symptoms of brain fog, fatigue or gut issues may subside. They key is to focus on getting your gut back on track and creating a balanced internal environment, like we discussed in the last section, then introducing egg back in.

Minor Triggers:

Intolerances to preservatives and additives are a little more difficult to notice. These are the numbers that you see on the back of packaged food. Even some of the naturally-occurring preservatives and additives can be detrimental to mood and behaviour – particularly for children. Because these additives and preservatives are not food, we're not designed to consume them. Our bodies go to a lot of effort to get them out of our system and it puts an undue stress on our adrenal glands and other organs. Reactions to these can result in wheeze, difficulty breathing, behavioural reactions, mood changes, fatigue, even ticks and tremors. A full list of ones to avoid can be found on page 103.

And lastly, this brings us to amines and salicylates – things that make food taste better, or more intense, or used to preserve. Amines are often found in cured meats and smoked foods, whereas high concentrations of salicylates naturally occur in some foods such as chocolate, peppermint tea, strawberries, oranges, lemons and tomatoes. If you have a salicylate sensitivity, you'll often notice a difference when it comes to fatigue patterns and gastrointestinal issues if you go without. Relief from bloating, flatulence, burping, reflux, heartburn, loose stools, constipation.

Detox

I'm sure you've heard of the term 'detoxing' before and perhaps you've even tried a detox yourself, but now we will delve into the science behind it and how we can detox our liver, our lives, our relationships and our energy.

This is great for anybody's irritable bowel syndrome (IBS) issues and those who may have had intolerances in the past. We'll also be exploring your mind-gut connection and how that affects your energy and your adrenal glands.

So, why detoxify? Detoxification isn't really something new. Cleansing has been around for at least 2,000 years and has its history in Ayurvedic and Chinese medicine. Regular detoxification has always been used as a means to optimise health and wellbeing. Modern life has us increasingly exposed to different toxic compounds in the air, the water and the food we eat. So we're not just getting it from one place, we're constantly bombarded by them wherever we go.

A symptom that you may feel from being a little bit toxic is that overwhelming feeling of being tired or lack of energy. That's why it's an important starting point for anyone trying to gain more energy out of their life. There's also headaches, recurrent infection, sensitivities, difficulty shifting weight, hormone irregularities like our adrenal hormones, PMS, psoriasis, acne and autoimmunity, which have all been associated with under-functioning detoxification pathways.

The liver

The liver is where all of your adrenalin and cortisol gets processed, so it's an integral part in dealing with adrenal fatigue. This goes hand-in-hand with your gut and how it's functioning. It's important that we are absorbing all of the nutrients that your adrenals require and making sure all the toxins are removed.

Every toxin and every compound that you are exposed to during your day – good, bad or ugly – is going to eventually make it into your blood stream and then through your detoxification pathways. And 25% of that is done through your gastrointestinal system, better known as your gut. The other 75% is all left up to your liver.

There are a couple of different processes that have to happen in your liver to make sure that your toxins get out. Specific toxins take specific pathways. Just before all that happens though, your liver and spleen filter the large majority of your blood cells. About 1.5 to 2.0 litres of blood passes through your liver per minute. We've only got about 6 to 8 litres in total, depending on if you're an adult female or male and in about three minutes all the blood within your body should be processed. It's like a big carwash. Blood coming from your intestines with bacterial endotoxins, or with toxins from good bacteria, all need to be processed and car-washed off the outside of those red blood cells.

Immune complexes – so if you're having a response to different foods or an autoimmune disorder – also needs to be processed. Other toxins that are coming in from your gut also need to be car-washed off. If that's not working as quickly as it should, then you're going to end up with those symptoms of fatigue, headaches, brain fog and sensitivity.

Bile is another way that your liver helps to remove toxic substances. Your liver makes about a litre of bile per day and that bile eventually turns into poo. Bile plus fibre equals poo. If your poo's aren't getting processed or being excreted out of your body, or if you're not getting enough fibre to make those poo's properly, then the toxins won't bind to them, they'll be reabsorbed back into circulation and have to be processed again.

Your Liver

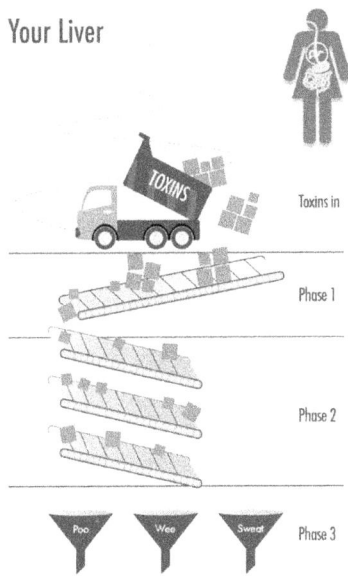

Toxins in

Phase 1

Phase 2

Phase 3

So when those toxins do come through your liver, it's a bit like going through a big factory, where the doors open up at around 2 to 4 o'clock in the morning. This is when most of our detoxification and liver regeneration happens – and it also happens to be when most of my clients say that they get up and do a wee. In actual fact, what is happening is that they're offloading toxins before the processing begins. This might be an indicator of overload and is not ideal for your body.

The toxins that we're talking about are internal toxins, external toxins and things that you probably even haven't thought about before.

Externally, everybody knows of toxins such as cigarette smoke, fumes from carbon monoxide, glues and cleaning products. But with internal (ingested) toxins, lots of people think about their liver and know all about the effect of alcohol or pharmaceutical drugs. But the other internal ones that you may not have thought of include preservatives and additives in your foods, the fats that you ingest whilst you're eating your dinner, the fats that you've got stored in your body, as well as your estrogen, your testosterone and your adrenalin. The reason why you don't stay hyperactive all the time, or the reason you don't stay stressed all the time, is because that adrenalin and other hormones are actually broken down into smaller pieces by your liver and processed through that detoxification mechanism.

So back to our factory, when those trucks that have picked up all of the toxins throughout your body arrive at the factory doors at 2 am, what happens is that it signals you to wake up to do a wee – essentially offloading all of the current toxins that have already been processed in your body, ready for the next batch to go through the factory.

So the truck turns up with a new batch of toxins, which then get offloaded onto a big conveyor belt. That conveyor belt is actually known as Phase I detoxification. Everything gets loaded on there and, in the general Western diet, what will happen is that Phase I generally goes quite quickly. Caffeine, alcohol and pharmaceutical medications tend to also speed it up.

What now happens is that a number of pathways – kind of like robotic arms – start to pull apart really large toxins into their smaller, much more toxic components. A lot of us think alcohol is bad? But alcohol dehydrogenase, which is the really small version of it, is highly, highly toxic. That's the reason people get hangovers. Because alcohol has been pulled apart to its smaller and more highly toxic component – alcohol dehydrogenase – which hasn't had enough time to move safely out of phase 2 of our system by the time we wake up in the morning, so we feel rubbish because it is not completely processed.

For Phase I to work correctly it needs all the B vitamins, amino acids, magnesium, glutathione, antioxidants, folate, fat-soluble vitamins, vitamin E and vitamin C. Now, if Phase I is going quite quickly due to the standard Western diet and lifestyle and isn't regulated by the required vitamins and minerals, we end up with lots of these smaller, highly toxic components quite quickly. Unfortunately, the next little set of conveyor belts, called Phase II, generally can't keep up with the demand from the first conveyor belt.

It is the job of Phase II to repackage up these toxins and remove them from the body. If Phase II is slowing right down, you'll end up with a backlog of these toxins at the end of Phase I which don't quite make it into Phase II – or those second conveyor belts – in the way that they need to be, in unison, to get them out of your body. If your Phase II is a little on the slow side, you'll be experiencing things like hormone disruption, toxicity and brain fog and won't be able to concentrate.

Phase II is generally slower in the Western diet due to deficiencies in vitamin B2, B5, B12 glutathione, zinc and vitamin C. Low protein diets will also slow down Phase II. Often people who've gone from being meat eaters to vegetarians will have a period of detoxification because they aren't getting the protein that they're used to.

Pharmaceutical medications such as ibuprofen, naproxen and aspirin will also slow down Phase II.

Things that can speed up Phase II, however, include vegetables from the brassica family such as broccoli and brussel sprouts, sulfurous foods, turmeric, citrus fruits such as lemons, caraway, folate, fish oil, B vitamins and amino acids such as glutamine, lysine, taurine and cysteine.

After Phase II, your toxins are repackaged up so that they're nice and safe to get out of your body. They then head to the poo chute, the wee chute, or the sweat chute. This is the way that we transfer them out of our body, or out of that factory, and get them out of our system.

It's interesting to note that the sweat chute – through your skin – eliminates heavy metals, lead and some pesticides which are toxic substances that come from your environment. If it's coming through your skin, sometimes you can have issues with skin conditions.

Generally, in between Phase I and Phase II, if you have a buildup of highly toxic metabolites, your body tries to do the best it can to keep those toxins away from you and keep you safe. Therefore hormones like estrogen or toxins like nicotine can get stored in your fat cells. Scientifically that's the best place for them. They're stored away. They're kept nice and safe from your body. The issue there is that if the detoxification pathway isn't working properly and you've stored the highly toxic metabolites in your fat cells, but you want to lose some weight in the form of fat, your body is going to do absolutely everything it can to keep you safe. So it's going to keep those fat cells on you as long as it possibly can so that the toxins don't come out. The cool thing about detoxifying, or making sure that those conveyor belts are working in unison, and having all of those wonderful vitamins and nutrients in there, is that your body can then be happy to let go of that weight for you.

Additionally, if that little pathway in between Phase I and Phase II gets overloaded, those toxins can go back into circulation. They're put back on the trucks the next night and have to go through the whole process again. This is not only tiring for your liver, but it can cause fatigue, weight gain and headaches. It can have flow on effects for a number of things that may have you feeling not quite right. Making sure those detoxification pathways work and getting all of those toxins out of your body is essential.

In the resources section on page 152 you can access the 7 Day Detox Protocol I use for so many of my clients to reset their livers and start with a clean slate.

Toxins

We're completely bombarded by different toxins in our lives, toxins such as stress. The physiological response to that is actually quite toxic for our bodies and has to be processed through the detoxification pathways in our liver. Some of our food choices, particularly the fast foods, are toxic in that they have preservatives, additives and a whole bunch of chemicals. In actual fact, about 700 man-made chemicals have been created since 1960.

Smoking is another one of the most detrimental toxins that we're bombarded with. Second-hand smoke does just as much damage. And when we're talking about environmental toxins, well, anything that's in your kitchen or cleaning cupboard could be an issue too.

We also have pharmaceutical medications. Relative to the history of the human body, these medications are made up of all new chemicals and a human body isn't quite used to dealing with these. Most people are not actually reacting to the active ingredient in that tablet, but the metabolite – the breakdown products. Our livers have to do a whole bunch of work to break them down to the active ingredient, which is then able to work on our body. Then we have to detoxify the active ingredient as well.

So what are we really talking about when we define a toxin? Toxins are defined as a compound that has a detrimental effect on cell function and structure. What that means is the actual function of the cells and how it's doing all of its processes, how the messages are getting out, how it goes about its business on a day-to-day basis and the structure for how it's built. Anything that damages that or has a detrimental effect on that is considered a toxin.

Most toxins can be defined into three different subcategories.

The first is heavy metals which are things mostly in our environment, things that we are getting from the outside world. The most common of these being cadmium, mercury, lead and arsenic, identified by the World Health Organisation to be of public concern.

The next subcategory is liver toxins. This is a combination of things that we're consuming and things that are inside us already – endotoxins and exotoxins. They need to be processed specifically by our liver cells, also known as hepatocytes.

The third toxin subcategory is microbial compounds. That's from bacteria and how they live on us, in us, how they die, and what they excrete – which all has to be detoxified by our bodies. Given we actually carry around about nine times more bacteria on us and in us than our human cells, this is very important!

Heavy metals

Lead, mercury, cadmium, arsenic, nickel and aluminium are all heavy metals. They're found in our environment and about 25% of the population is affected by heavy metal toxicity. That's one in four people who have a load higher than the recommended dose of heavy metals within their body. Heavy metals are very, very difficult for your body to process, so they get stored in different areas of your body. Some are in fat cells, which makes it difficult to detoxify because you end up having a toxic load of heavy metals coming out when you're trying to lose weight. Our body is doing the best it can to protect us from these toxic metals by storing them away, so it will do the best it can to avoid them getting out. This makes it much more difficult to lose weight. And some of them are deposited in the brain, which is a whole big lump of fat in itself – it's about 80% fat and a whole bunch of water. Aluminium, in particular, is deposited in the brain and has been associated with Alzheimer's and early onset dementia.

Hair mineral analysis is the best way to check for heavy metal toxicity. There is also a urine test that you can do. Unfortunately for some of us, including myself, that have artificially coloured hair, you're going to get some weird and wacky results. You need to have at least three centimetres of regrowth so that they can catch the portion of the hair that isn't affected by the other metals and minerals that are in your hair dye.

Most heavy metals come from our environment. Lead can be present in spray bottles, cooking utensils and tin cans. In fact, tin cans used to be lined with lead.

Mercury is in amalgam dental fillings, which a lot of people know about. It's also high in contaminated fish and you can also find it in cosmetics. It's really important to look not just at the ingredients in your food, but the outside of your cosmetics, your shampoos, your conditioners and anything that you're actually putting on your skin. The rules for labelling cosmetics allow the manufacturers to leave off mercury if it is less than 65 parts per million, so a little research is required on your part to find out if your skin cream or powder has it in it.

The skin is the largest organ in your body. It absorbs pretty much everything from the environment and it also expels things from your body. It's your largest organ of excretion as well. When you consider the amount of beauty products you use on any given morning, you're mixing a cocktail of chemicals on your skin. Which means you could be having chemical reactions occurring that also need to be detoxified via your liver.

Aluminium is another heavy metal that is found in cosmetics like deodorant. One of the most mind-boggling things for me to comprehend is that people are putting aluminium straight under their armpits. Your armpits are the place we find the most lymphatic tissue. And the lymph is the most well known pathway that cancer travels and spreads. So, we're putting heavy metals directly on the largest lymph area of our body, daily, and not even thinking twice about it. If you have a look at your deodorant, and aluminium is one of the first three ingredients – or it may be listed as the active ingredient, which is usually located on the front of the product – you may want to choose a new deodorant. The aluminium build-up can happen within the lymph. It can also happen within fat cells. It can happen all over the place and the detrimental effects are well documented. Over the counter antacid medications also have aluminium in them. Even cookware, at certain temperatures, can denature its own aluminium and it will end up in your food, which is then deposited all over your body. Swapping these products out of your home for one without aluminium is the first step and detoxifying is the second.

Some signs that you might have a toxic load of heavy metals include headaches that you can't find the cause of, fatigue, muscle pain, joint pain, indigestion, tremors, constipation, anaemia, pallor (which is a pasty-white kind of colour to your skin), and poor coordination and concentration. It's also been linked with ADHD, Obsessive compulsive disorder (OCD), Alzheimer's, Parkinson's and other neurological disorders. There have been quite a number of clients that come into the clinic with tremors and even Tourette Syndrome, and we've tested for heavy metal toxicity and found that at least one or more of those has been contributing to the current situation.

If you feel that you're suffering from heavy metal toxicity, there are some great nutrients that can combat them. If we're only having small amounts of these heavy metals coming into our body day-in and day-out, what we can do is ensure that we have small amounts of the foods that help process these metals out of our bodies. Water-soluble fibre is one of the best recommendations for this. Foods like guar gum, oats, pectin, chia seeds, LSA (linseed, sunflower and almond meal) and psyllium can bind to the heavy metals and get them out via our poo.

Heavy metals are detoxified by a pathway in our liver called sulfation. Sulfation needs sulfur to work, which is present in foods such as garlic, onions and eggs. Bear in mind that the ones that are the smelliest are the best ones for binding to heavy metals.

Vitamins C and B are also important cofactors to detoxify heavy metals as well. Other minerals like calcium, magnesium, zinc, iron, copper and chromium also chelate or balance out the heavy metals and how they're removed from your body. The last amazing chelating food is coriander (cilantro). Coriander is absolutely spectacular at heavy metal detoxification and can be used in your cooking or in juices.

Liver toxins

Liver toxins are comprised of anything that goes through our liver cells to be processed. Toxic chemicals can come from internal sources and can also be ingested. So, the ingested ones, things like alcohol, drugs (both pharmaceutical and recreational), solvents, formaldehyde, pesticides, and food additives and preservatives, are all going to make their way into our body and thus, our liver. Those that are internal, the different fats, they all end up being processed through the liver cells also. Fatty acids, like those found in canola or vegetable oil which have been overcooked – the denatured versions of fat – are not only detrimental to your cardiovascular system, but they're also detrimental to your liver and have to be processed there too. I recently read a study about how the FDA (Food and Drug Administration in the U.S.A.) has just put forward a bill to completely ban trans-fatty acids in cooking and food because of such a high risk of cardiovascular disease and, in the long term, killing people.

Saturated fats also have to go through the liver, as well as hormones like estrogen, testosterone, dopamine and adrenalin. How many people aren't aware that their liver does this huge, massive job for them? Absolutely everything you get exposed to, including your own hormones, has to be processed by your liver to be eliminated.

Stress also affects the toxic load on your liver. When we think of stressors, we think of them as mostly psychological and neurological. When you notice that you have a high load or an increasing amount of liver toxins, you may notice that you're having issues with depression, headache, mental confusion or brain fog, some forms of mental illness, tingling hands and feet, abnormal nerve reflexes, sensitivity to chemicals or irregular reactions to drugs. Speaking of drug reactions, when clients come in who are having an abnormal reaction to a pharmaceutical medication – if their doctor has given them medication and it's supposed to have done one thing but ends up doing something else or they have an interesting side effect to it – often there is an issue with their liver not being able to process that drug properly. This can be genetic or functional and there are a number of tests your health practitioner can perform to find out if this is the case for you.

Optimising liver detoxification means eating a diet based on fresh fruit and vegetables, whole grains, legumes, nuts and seeds. You'll notice that all these things come from plants – they are the best natural detoxifiers. Phytochemicals, all the wonderful nutrients that are available in plants, are exactly what we need to process toxins in the liver. Generally, a human body is designed to process this out; it's designed to be optimal when you're consuming four of your own handfuls of plant-based material.

The easiest and most practical way to find out whether you are consuming enough plants for optimal liver function is to create a cup shape with your hands. You need four 'cups' per day. But every hand size is different – your kids' hands are going to be much smaller, for example. This is why it is such a good gauge – it's a built-in measurement as to how much you need based on your size.

Within the 7-day detox protocol, you'll notice that the first two days are purely plant based. This is to make sure that you're getting all the nutrients you absolutely need. Then we reintroduce things like lighter proteins, followed by harder, more difficult to breakdown proteins over the last couple of days. This leaves you feeling lighter, with more energy, less sluggish and with better sleep.

Toning exercise down is another really important thing to do. You'll notice in the seven-day detox that there is either walking or gentle, non-competitive movement every single day for 20 minutes. This pumps all of the toxins through your liver and also increases your lymphatic load of getting toxins out. Also, avoiding alcohol and caffeine is hugely important to the liver if you're planning on detoxifying it.

Taking a multivitamin would be one of my biggest suggestions as well. This is because we often don't consume the required amounts of vitamins and nutrients on a daily basis, and the mineral content in our soils isn't the same as it used to be back in our grandparents' era. So taking a high quality multivitamin really supports your liver while it's trying to do its best to detoxify that backlog. Using specialised nutritional supplements can sometimes help as well. Notice that my detox plan includes suggestions of St Mary's Thistle, Dandelion and Schisandra which are generally available at health food stores. Those three major herbs tend to work on helping your liver detoxify.

Regular detoxification through juicing or supplementation, fasting or detox protocols can really help. Regular usually means twice a year, and I generally do this twice a year myself. The best times that I've found to detox is in Spring – getting back on track after Winter, cleaning out all of that stuff that may have gone into overdrive over the year, gaining a fresh new outlook – and also after Christmas and New Year celebrations, once the silly season is over. The silly season can be quite a dodgy time for food, as well as being higher in fat and a bit more difficult to process.

Microbial compounds

The third subcategory of toxins are microbial compounds. Microbial compounds is a term that covers anything that is bacterial, including our own microbes. This is a pretty big component of toxins, as humans have approximately 100,000 times more bacteria than average human DNA. That means we're actually all a bunch of microbes carrying around a human, not a human carrying a bunch of microbes. So they play a major role in what's happening on us and in us. Fortunately, they also have a lifecycle.

These microbes go around chewing, consuming and contributing to different things that are happening throughout our body. But they also produce their own by-products – toxins – which are released into your gut and need to be absorbed and then processed by our liver. The compounds that come from these little microbes are called exotoxins (excreted externally) and endotoxins (contained inside the microbe). As mentioned before, microbes have a life cycle and when they die, the endotoxins burst out and end up in our system where they need to be processed.

These microbial compounds are also implicated in liver

disease, Crohn's disease, neurotransmitter issues, lupus, pancreatitis, allergies, asthma and autoimmune reactions. Therefore making sure that you process these properly will lessen your chances of having these toxic disorders.

Testing

To find out if you are truly toxic, apart from the signs and symptoms, is to undertake a liver function test (LFT) by your doctor. It's a bit of a misnomer though. It's not actually telling you the function of your liver – it's telling you the byproducts that are floating around in your serum, which doesn't really have anything to do with your liver at all. LFTs are a great way of finding out whether you should be hospitalised or not for your liver function, it is a general pathology test and is performed by all Doctors. But, the actual *function* of your liver is best tested by a Functional Liver Detoxification Profile (FLDP). It gives you information on the different stages of your liver processes and if they are optimal or not. This test can be ordered by your integrative health practitioner through a functional pathology laboratory.

If bloating, flatulence, loose stools, constipation or a history of medication, alcohol or stress ending in gut symptoms is an issue then CDSA might help. The complete digestive stool analysis, or CDSA, is another functional laboratory test that tells you about all of the different microbes that are growing in your gastrointestinal lining. It'll show up with any bad stuff like parasites, bacterium and different yeast strains, and it'll also tell you about good guys, the ones that are keeping everything under control for you. Additionally, great clinical questioning from your health practitioner around your lifestyle factors can usually determine what's going on for your liver.

How to help our liver detoxify

Our liver thrives on certain nutrients to help it process efficiently. Curcumin, which is the active ingredient in turmeric, is fantastic for the liver and is something you can easily purchase from a health food shop. Then we have all our B vitamins, magnesium, sufficient zinc and sufficient vitamin C. But there are also some key dietary and lifestyle points that can really give the liver a head start.

Protein:

Eggs are a fantastic source of protein, although protein doesn't have to come from an animal form. There are many other options such as chickpeas, kidney beans, black beans, tofu and soybeans – but they all need to be eaten with a grain to get the complete benefit. Tofu is from soybeans and traditionally goes well with rice. Chickpeas, which is what hummus is made from, goes quite well with pita bread which is made from wheat. Then you've got your Mexican food – you can start with kidney beans mixed with a corn tortilla. If you're a vegetarian and worried about the amount of protein that you're having through the detoxification, you just need to make sure that you are protein combining to get the full complement of amino acids.

Fats:

Good fats can be extremely beneficial when detoxing. These can include cold-pressed or extra-virgin oils like coconut, rice bran, olive oil and nut oils like sesame or macadamia. And don't forget probiotics, which are going to help release the nasty bacteria that may or may not be growing in your system.

Fibre:

One of the most important things to have within your diet is water-soluble fibre. Fibrous foods like vegetables, guar gum, pectin, grated apple, oat bran (actually anything with the word bran on the end of it has soluble fibre), psyllium, LSA and chia seeds are all very high in soluble fibre. They have the ability to bind to toxins within the gut, promote their excretion and get them out nice and safely. Without chewing properly, there is no way your body is going to get toxins out. Those toxins will stay inside you, get reabsorbed and you'll then have to reprocess them. It can be an exhausting situation for your body. Making sure you have enough fibre and that you're chewing properly is essential.

But remember that if you're concentrating on an optimal detox, consuming adequate water is essential for getting those water soluble toxins out of your body, around two litres of water as a minimum per day is needed.

Water:

Water is hugely essential for releasing toxins. If you're not used to having water, here are ten tips that may help:

1. You need about 33ml of water per kilogram of body weight, every day. Therefore if you weigh 60 kilograms, that's about 1.9 litres. If you're higher than that, then you're going to be over that two litre mark.

2. Drinking the best quality water that you can find. This doesn't mean going out and buying some really big, expensive filter. We're very lucky that in Australia we are blessed with very clean water, albeit some places can be higher in different types of chemicals, like fluoride. But we don't have too much of a chance of microbe contamination that could cause illness outbreaks.

So it's about finding the best water that you can. It may be buying bottled water, or you might purchase a filter jug to keep in your fridge. Or it could be getting a copper filter or a clay filter. Any of those types would be beneficial to making sure that you have the cleanest possible water you can. In most western countries in the presence of none of those filters, having boiled tap water is better than not having any water at all.

3. Avoid diuretic beverages. That means coffee and tea – although tea is less diuretic than coffee by about two thirds. Having two cups of tea per day is sufficient when you're on your detox, and herbal teas are preferable. It's ideal to stay away from black tea and coffee for the week that you're doing the detox.

4. Drink 300mls of water as part of your detox protocol with lemon in the morning to alkalise. If you don't have fresh lemons, then squeezed lemon in a bottle will do.

5. Drink at regular intervals. Don't wait until you're thirsty. There is this fantastic water bottle from motivationalbottle.com which graduates in timings on the side of the bottle so that you know how much you should have been drinking at certain times of the day. I think its genius in making sure that you regularly drink.

6. Get a nice water bottle and carry it with you. One of the biggest things that I've noticed about mums that come into my clinic is that they've got the best water bottles in the world for their kids, yet they don't have one for themselves. It's nice to have nice things. You can get fairly cheap, large, Bisphenol A (BPA) read: nasty toxic plasticiser free, stainless steel water bottles from supermarkets, health food stores or online. When we are carrying them, and they're an accessory, it's more likely that you're going to use them.

7. Create a habit out of drinking water. Aim to drink a certain amount before lunch or before you leave work. Also, having a certain amount every week is going to slowly increase your threshold for the amount of water that you can drink. Generally, we find ourselves at a stage where our body feels as though we don't need water, but if we have 600ml per day for one week and then stop, we start to notice signs of thirst. Your nervous system redefines what your balance is so that you're not triggered by the thirst reflex all the time. If we then double our intake the next week to 1.2 litres, our bodies can handle the gradual increase without wanting to wee all the time. But then, if you take a day off from drinking water, you'll get the signs and symptoms of dehydration – dry mouth, dry skin, and things will be a bit itchier than usual.

8. Increasing your water when your mental activity increases as well as your physical activity. You will go through the same processes. Your body doesn't know the difference between physical, mental or emotional. It's still going to be processing quite quickly and it's going to need water for all those chemical processes to work.

9. Drink more water through fresh juices or smoothies. It doesn't just have to be straight water, although it is preferable that the majority is through water.

10. Sweat. Have a sauna, hot bath, or exercise to the point of perspiration, and drink sufficient water before and after. When it comes to water and balancing your body, sweating once per week is essential for getting toxins out of your skin. So exercising to the point of sweating, or being in a hot bath or a sauna is hugely beneficial during detox.

Minimising Added Sugars:

Not a lot of people know that, if you add two glucose (sugar) molecules together, you actually end up with cholesterol through a little process called glycogen synthesis. Cholesterol is processed by your liver. The higher sugar content you have, the more likely you are to be having an issue with your liver. Minimise added sugars in your life, like sugars in your teas or fizzy drinks. You may not notice that other drinks also have added sugars in them, such as flavoured milk. But the big offenders are the soft drinks. Making sure that you cut added sugars is really important on the week that you do your detox. But sugar doesn't just add to your toxic load – it also changes your mood. It stimulates your cortisol and thus affects your adrenal glands. It changes the balance with which your body deals with cortisol – it basically stresses out your body as soon as you consume it. Now, don't get me wrong, natural sugars in whole fruit are fantastic for your body. But if you take the straight sugar out of fruit, called fructose, and repackage it as a soft drink, it has very detrimental effects for both your adrenal glands and your pancreas to be able to balance out your blood sugar.

Non-toxic cooking:

Toxic cooking includes the radiation that comes from microwaves. Microwaves also alter some of the phytochemicals that are in our food. The worst thing you can do in a microwave, though, is use plastic wrap. If you use plastic wrap when cooking or reheating in a microwave, you may have noticed the plastic wrap actually melts. That melting plastic goes into your body and has to be processed. It's a very, very difficult thing for your body to do. There is a reason we don't eat plastic in our diet, it's not food!

It is also good to be aware that oil has a smoking point. The second your oil starts smoking, it has transformed those fats into trans-fatty acids. Whenever it's smoking, you're actually consuming carcinogens, cancer-causing agents. Oils have different smoking points or a different heat point where they start to turn into trans-fatty acids. Rice bran oil has one of the highest temperatures, so it's best to do stir-fries and similar meals in this oil.

Re-using oil is also another point to be aware of. If you strain and re-use oil, you will need to consider the oxidation process – what happens when it sits out in the open air. It goes rancid on a micro level. Rancid oil is very difficult for your body to process and is laden with free-radicals. Free radicals cause a cellular mess that needs to be cleaned up by your body. So, re-using oil is another no-no.

Beware of charring your meat – whether this is on a barbecue or in a frypan. Charcoal is actually a carcinogen, a cancer-causing agent, and not something you want your body to have to detoxify.

Steaming is one of the best ways to look after your food. You'll generally keep the available vitamin content and you won't denature all the wonderful phytochemicals in your food.

Stir-frying is another great option. This is a quick method of cooking your food to maintain the maximum amount of those vitamins and nutrients in there. Just remember to use an oil with a high smoke point, such as rice bran oil, coconut or macadamia.

Exercise:

Exercise, making sure that you get that blood pumping regularly, is going to change the way that your body detoxifies. During the seven-day detox protocol, you'll notice that I suggest 20 minutes every day. It doesn't have to be crazy, heart-pumping stuff. We can have gentle, non-competitive movement too. But you do need to get your heart rate up at some point.

Sleep:

Sleep is essential for detoxification. If you're having issues with sleep, particularly if one to four o'clock in the morning is your toughest time, then that needs to be addressed. We need to make sure that sleep is working so that all the essential rejuvenation can happen and your body can process toxins before you wake up in the morning. Your body can't possibly deal with stress, deal with energy lulls or deal with detoxification issues if you're not sleeping well. It rejuvenates all of your cells by the time you wake up in the morning.

Sleep, or lack of it is the number one biggest contributing factor to long term stress and adrenal fatigue. It has negative implications for your entire body.

- Establish and maintain a regular time for going to bed and rising. (Rising at the same time is important) Best to retire no later than 10 pm for your adrenals.

- Expose yourself to bright light/sunlight in the morning.

- No caffeine after lunch/2pm as it has a half life of 8 hours.

- Avoid drinking soft drinks, as they will spike your cortisol.

- See a Chiropractor/Osteopath for neck adjustment.

- Eat light meals at night, as your body needs to use its energy to rejuvenate itself rather than spend the night digesting food you have just eaten.

- Dim the lights at night turn on low watt lamps and turn down the TV and electronic devices.

- Avoid Tyramine foods (aged, cured, meats and cheeses) after 5pm.

- Avoid eating starches after 5pm (the carbohydrate being digested will give you a spike in cortisol).

- Eat seasonal fruits.

- Make sure the bedroom is completely dark and free from noise (consider ear plugs, eye mask, block out curtains) also consider removing or covering brightly lit alarm clocks.

- Create a sleep-promoting environment that is comfortable (cool, quiet and dark).

- Avoid using an electric blanket (or warm up then unplug from wall).

- Electrical appliances and mobile phones should be at a distance of one metre or more from bed (subtle electromagnetic fields can affect your sleep).

- Avoid watching TV in bed and using electronic devices in bed, in fact avoid spending time in bed other than when actually sleeping.

- Avoid exercising too late at night (you want to slow your body down, not speed it up).

- "Power Nap" 20 minutes around 2pm if needed.

- Nasal breathing is essential/close your mouth. Breathing nasal strips can open up nasal passages if required and can be purchased from a pharmacy.

- Establish a regular bedtime routine/ritual so that you start to connect these pre-bed activities (such as a bath, listening to certain music, cup or herbal tea or low sugar hot chocolate) with a winding-down sensation, and then doing them or even thinking about them will make you feel relaxed and sleepy.

- Learn ways to manage stress. Consider talking to a counsellor / life coach / yoga, also try playing meditation / relaxation / hypnosis CDs an hour before bed.

During your sleep you will make hormones, detoxify your liver (between 1 and 3 am), recharge your brain and renew your immunity, so good quality sleep is VITAL.

The biggest challenge is to try not to worry about your lack of sleep, as this just creates extra pressure on you to fall asleep, perpetuating insomnia.

Environment:

It's essential for you to look at the ingredient panels on the things that you're putting in, on and around you. SLS, which is sodium laurel sulfate or sodium laureth sulfate, is used in foaming cleaning products. It will be used in your shampoos, conditioners and other agents such as liquid hand wash. If SLS is in the top three ingredients then it can be associated with cancer-causing compounds. It's ideal to find products that don't have SLS on the ingredient panel.

Parabens, or anything with the word *paraben* on the end of it, disrupts hormone function. Parabens are also found in shampoo, conditioner, moisturisers and soaps. Another ingredient to avoid is petroleum distillates. This can be present in cosmetics like lip balms, lipstick and moisturisers, and can be toxic. Even paw-paw ointment can have a petroleum distillate in it. You wouldn't drink petrol so putting it on your skin isn't the best thing for you either.

We also need to look at detoxifying your home. You need to make sure that the toxic load at home isn't going to cause problems when it comes to you keeping your family or yourself healthy. Making sure that the air is fresh and ensuring that you don't have an increased amount of dust, mould, cockroaches or animal dander build up is essential to prevent your body from reacting to these extra environmental toxins. Spring cleaning is a fantastic way of decreasing the toxic load in your environment.

Now we come to plastics. Anything that is made of plastic, which isn't BPA free, is toxic. You might look around your home and find water bottles that aren't BPA free, drink bottles, storage containers, kitchen wrap, and even plasticisers in your nail polish – all of which may disrupt hormones. Try to go BPA free where possible to reduce the toxic load.

Do you purchase new clothes and wear them without washing them first? Think again, not only for hygiene reasons, but because the plastic that they're shipped in is toxic. That plastic is usually full of BPA. There also may be mould or dust spores along with all sorts of irritants from the environment that get held underneath the plastic. Those plastic smells that are in your fresh, new sheets or your new clothes are actually toxic – your sense of smell is trying to tell you this. The closer your clothes and bedding are to organic, natural and eco-friendly, the better. If you can smell it then it's also being ingested by your mouth, nose, eyes and skin. Just think about how many toxins you are ingesting by simply walking down the laundry or the cleaning aisle of your local supermarket!

Which brings us to cleaning products. Cleaners that you might have underneath your kitchen sink or in your laundry or even in your bathroom, need to be non-toxic. If there are too many numbers or chemical words on your cleaning products then perhaps reconsider purchasing them again. There are so many non-toxic cleaning products on the market these days, so when it's time to replace your cleaning products, consider purchasing a safer version or making your own.

Detoxifying your house, in a nutshell, means to stop buying things that contain chemicals and synthetics. Avoid chemicals in ingredient lists and words 'derived from' or 'nature identical,' because they're not from nature. They're just *synthetically similar* to nature. Its great marketing!

Mindset

The last major contribution to our toxicity is our mindset. Detoxifying your emotions, detoxifying relationships and detoxifying your mindset is a huge part in making sure that you don't have anything standing in the way of your success when it comes to your energy.

Your liver is located around your body's third energy centre, or chakra. I don't generally talk about energy centres, but your third chakra is your emotional centre, where your solar plexus is located. Issues at this centre usually revolve around taking care of yourself rather than everybody else – putting yourself first. It's all about body acceptance and self-esteem, which is often what I find is happening for my clients. If you have these types of issues arising, you need to clear your mindset.

Patterns caused by destructive choices that are particular to your liver are emotions like anger, frustration, rage, jealousy and guilt. Some of these emotions may come up when you detoxify. Frustration is a common one that I find I'm personally affected by whenever I do a detox. Generally, on the second or third day, my husband will notice and ask if I'm on my detox because I have a tendency towards being quick to snap and experience anger. These do pass and after the detox you'll be left feeling on top of the world.

A quick tip from the *Access Consciousness* program and two of my favourite questions to ask are, *how does it get any better than this* and *what else is possible?*

I use the question *how does it get any better than this?*

When I'm stuck in the anger, it's a really quick and easy way for me to take a moment to think about a different outcome.

Toxic Relationships:

Toxic relationships are also a major issue for most women when it comes to their partners, their families or their friends. There may be someone in that group or that circle that is a major energy sucker.

How on earth do you think you're going to get more energy if you're allowing somebody else to take up your time and your space?

It's a very valuable commodity and allowing that is very detrimental to your health. One of the questions that I ask myself is, *is this rewarding and will it contribute to my life?*

Then I wait for the feeling, and make a choice. Now, that feeling is the one that we talked about previously during the Values exercise.

For instance, recently I had some friends that were asking me to go to their place. They're friends from a long, long time ago that particularly like to drink, and particularly like doing things without their children. Now, I have a lot of clarity around my values when it comes to my family. I like doing things with my family on the weekend. I also don't particularly like excessive drinking anymore. I prefer great conversation and being around my family. So I sat there and I thought, okay, I haven't been to visit for a long time. But going to see them was going to be an energy suck. I would have to try and make conversation. And I would be sad that I wasn't with my family.

So I asked myself,

"Is this rewarding and will it contribute to my life?"

No, not really. It's not going to contribute to my life and I didn't get a good feeling about it. It wasn't a feeling I wanted to feel. So, as difficult as it was, I had to let them know I didn't want to go.

It felt like the world had been lifted off my shoulders and the relief was palpable.

Attitude of Gratitude:

One of the exercises in the seven-day detox is creating a journal. In that journal, even if you don't write anything else in it, I want you to write down the top three things that you're grateful for in the last 24 hours. If that's a little bit difficult, then try the last week. The more you can cultivate an attitude of gratitude, the easier life is, and the easier it is for your brain to look for that pattern of things to be grateful for. I do it every night and I absolutely love it.

Celebration:

After your detox, celebrating your body is really important. You have a body. It's with you all the time. It's just like having another pet or another child. But we tend to ignore it.

If it's giving you signs and symptoms, it's time to make sure you're listening and giving it the best possible help that you can. Doing a detox and then celebrating how clean and cleansed your body is by going for a massage or a bush walk, or whatever it happens to be for you that brings you that bliss, and really connecting with your body is a great way of celebrating the gift of health.

In summary, not only do you need to understand your body but also an awareness of your emotions.

Cleansing emotional stress, allows for healing on a deeper level, by exploring the negative stress from relationships with yourself and others.

Bringing in more positive emotions, relationships and processes into your life is an essential part of healing, and don't forget to celebrate your wins along the way.

Clean eating guide

I'm sure by now you've heard of the Paleo way of eating. It refers to the Paleolithic era where scientists believe that our human bodies, as they currently are biologically, were functioning at their best.

There is a big crossover between Paleo food and another term you may have heard – clean eating.

This refers to foods that are as close to nature as they can be. These days, however, many foods have been messed with which can upset your system or throw it out of balance. This includes fried, smoked and canned foods. The issue with canned foods is in the processing – not only do they need to be heated which affects their vitamin and mineral content, but they also leach minerals from the can itself into the food.

You may be interested to know that frozen foods are ok. Here in Australia they are quite high in vitamins and nutrients and can often contain more nutrients than fresh produce that may have been gassed or prematurely picked. Gassing fruit and vegetables allows them to look fresher for longer so they last on the shelves of the supermarkets.

Over-processed wheat is another issue, particularly due to genetic modification.

Unfortunately we've got a mono-culture here in Australia, which means there's only one specific strain that dominates the wheat industry because it isn't too affected by weather or insects. Signs or symptoms commonly associated with wheat intolerance can include itchy skin, psoriasis or dermatitis.

Other foods that have been tampered with include milk. Milk used to come from one cow, contain beneficial bacteria and usually consumed immediately. Whereas these days, one carton of milk can come from not only a multitude of cows, but a multitude of dairies. Then it's homogenised and pasteurised, killing off all the beneficial bacteria as well as the nasty bacteria so that it can be stored for a much longer period of time and consumed by anyone.

Like wheat, the overexposure to dairy can cause an issue in certain people, particularly those that have a lowered immune system or who are under a high amount of stress. This affects their gastrointestinal lining and can result in symptoms such as constipation or diarrhoea.

And whilst we're mentioning the stress aspect, some clean foods that may not cause an issue usually, can disrupt our system particularly after long periods of stress, adrenal fatigue and/or damaged gastrointestinal lining. Foods such as nuts, kale, buckwheat, cabbage and brussel sprouts – which are normally hugely beneficial for our hormone imbalances – can pose an issue if we've had long-term stress.

The more you follow the Paleo and clean eating guidelines, the better off you'll be and the less likely you will cause disruptions in your body.

Channeling your inner hunter-gatherer isn't as hard as it seems – start simply by shopping at your local farmers or fruit and vegetable markets. Plus the produce is more likely to be organic. There are so many different pesticides used these days, mainly to increase the amount of food that is produced. Unfortunately, these pesticides have other detrimental effects. So choose organic where possible but if you can't, rinsing the produce in some white vinegar and warm water will clear off most of the chemical residue.

And, of course, if you have the opportunity to grow your own fruit and vegetables, even better. You know how you have grown them. You know where they've come from. You know the effort that's gone into growing them. This a great project to get the kids involved in, too. Just like any other kids, mine don't necessarily eat all of the vegetables that I would like them to, but when they are involved in growing the vegetables – fertilizing them, watering them, tending to them – they tend to want to try them! There's a vested interest in what's actually going on.

So just do what you can, even if it's some herbs on your back verandah or in your kitchen. Having that connection with your food is going to change the way that you really think about and consume it.

What other foods do we include in the clean eating guidelines? Root vegetables are a must. Sweet potatoes, turnips, carrots and beetroot are all fantastic. Coconut has also come back into fashion as a superfood and has a wide range of uses, including popping it in your smoothies, cooking with coconut milk, and consuming the oil due to its good fat properties.

Organic meat is another one to include. This is meat that hasn't been tampered with, hasn't had any hormones put through it, has been raised in its natural environment and fed its natural diet.

Food labels

It is imperative to always read the nutritional label on your food. It's there for a reason and we have been lured into this false sense of security that everything on the food label is going to be good for us.

So, when checking out nutritional labels, you'll find that there are two panels. One is the nutritional panel, telling you how many macronutrients it contains. This covers protein, fats, carbohydrates, as well as a breakdown of the sugar content.

Sugars shouldn't be more than five grams per hundred. The second panel contains all the ingredients, which is where all the big, juicy information about the additives and preservatives are detailed.

If you are unsure of what the numbers mean or perhaps you've noticed that a particular one gives you a headache, there is usually a number that you can call on the back of the packet. Manufacturers must disclose information about the product and how it's been made.

Additive and intolerance resources

Some of the obstacles we have to our health have been sneakily put into our food. There's a lot of information out there about additives, but I've found Sue Dengate's work in *FedUp* to be the most comprehensive.

She's an Australian food technologist who has really checked out the different additives and preservatives in our foods. Some of the additives have an association with asthma, skin conditions, migraines, headaches, fatigue, brain fog, as well as some neurological conditions like tremors and Tourette Syndrome.

Nasty Additives to Avoid

Colours and Artificials

102 tartrazine	104 quinoline yellow
110 sunset yellow	122 azorubine, carmoisine
123 amaranth	124 ponceau, brilliant scarlet
127 erythrosine	129 allura red
132 indigotine, indigo carmine	133 brilliant blue
142 green S, food green, acid brilliant green	143 fast green FCF
151 brilliant black	155 brown, chocolate brown

Natural

160b annatto, bixin, norbixin

Preservatives

200-203 sorbic acid, potassium and calcium sorbates

210-213 benzoic acid, sodium, potassium and calcium benzoates

220-228 sulphur dioxide, all sulphites, bisulphites, metabisulphites

249-252 all nitrates and nitrites

280-283 propionic acid, sodium, potassium and calcium propionates

Synthetic Antioxidants

310-312 all gallates

319-321 TBHQ, BHA butylated hydroxyanisole, BHT butylated hydroxytoluene

Flavour Enhancers

620-625 glutamic acid and all glutamates, MSG monosodium glutamate

627 disodium guanylate

631 disodium inosinate

635 ribonucleotides

Yeast extract, HVP HPP hydrolysed vegetable or plant protein

There has been some clear scientific validation on this and she has collated a lot of empirical evidence from the stories of her clients, especially when it comes to children. Generally, to discover these reactions, clients are put on a very restrictive diet and then foods are re-introduced. The part of treatment that is missing is healing that force field that acts as our protective barrier, our gut lining.

The next fantastic Australian resource is the *Additive Free Pantry*. It's a shopping guide that you can take anywhere. You're able to check out the foods that don't have any additives in them, which is really good for anyone who has kids or who's having a hard time trying to find snacks that are beneficial for their body.

Another resource is *The Friendly Food Cookbook*, which comes from the Royal Prince Alfred Hospital in Sydney, Australia. It gives you a fantastic overview on how allergies and intolerances work, and how preservatives and additives are affecting our gastrointestinal lining and our immune system. It contains some great recipes but I particularly like the overview on intolerances.

There is one way to find out if you have any type of intolerance, be it to preservatives, additives, whole foods, or macro portions of foods which includes salicylates. The elimination diet is generally a six- to twelve-week program of slowly cutting out everything except for pears, lamb and potato. Even then, some people have reactions to those. It can be a very, very difficult road to go down to find out about your responses to foods but you can do a mini-version of it.

Through detoxing, you may have noticed the different reactions that your body has to certain foods – even after a short period of just one week. If your body has a response, be it a tummy thing, an upper respiratory tract thing, sinus, a bit stuffed up, or perhaps you notice more mucous than usual, then you have to trust in your body and take note of the reaction. It is a symptom; your body is trying to tell you what's going on. If we just tap in and listen, then it can be really beneficial in the long run.

Meal planning

"By failing to prepare, you are preparing to fail."

You might come up against some hiccups when changing some of the foods in your diet. And perhaps there may be some hesitancy with your partner or kids. The idea, particularly when it comes to attitudes and intolerances, is to plan ahead.

Now we're going to set up a process for you to get the most out of what you need for your adrenal glands to go from that feeling of burnt out, to all the energy you require. This is where meal plans and a little bit of preparation becomes essential to your ability to thrive.

Breakfast always needs to have a few vital components – the first is making sure you do have breakfast for starters! The next component is that your breakfast needs to contain some protein. Then we need to make sure that there is some form of fibre in it. Another component is having some form of plant in there which needs to fit into your lifestyle too.

Some other options for breakfast include eggs and vegetables or homemade baked beans.

The addition of plants to those options makes it a full complement of protein, plants and fibre – an ideal breakfast.

Lunch needs to be something that's going to sustain you through the afternoon. It's preferable not to have anything that's high glycemic index (GI) during lunch, otherwise you may need that afternoon nap. High GI foods are those that are high in sugars, such as carbohydrates. Lunch needs to have as much plant-based material in it as we can get, plus a good form of protein. So tuna, salmon, soup, beans if you're a vegetarian, and/or eggs depending on the type of intolerances you have. This mixed with salad is ideal. You could include all of those components in a wrap, but try to avoid bread as it won't sustain you during the afternoon.

The next meal is dinner. We need to make sure that we're getting a wide variety of foods at dinner time, making sure that we are plant passionate on our dinner plate, and having some form of protein as well. If you are going to have some form of carbohydrates, my suggestion is rice or gluten-free pasta and to have no more than a half cup of it, cooked. The reasoning behind this is the adrenal hormone cortisol is intricately connected to glucose. White starchy carbohydrates form glucose as they hit the blood stream which may have negative consequences for your adrenals late at night.

For snacks, we are looking at sundried fruit (not ones that are preserved in sulfur), peanuts, macadamias, walnuts, almonds, pepitas, sunflower seeds and popcorn. All of these are high fibre and low GI, with lasting energy that will sustain you throughout the day. Yoghurt is another snack that would be really beneficial to have, again choose the lowest in sugar for adrenal health.

We can even make some energy / protein balls which would be great too. The general recipe is made up of dates, dried nuts/seeds or coconut in a food processor.

Here's my favourite recipe:

- 300g made up of dried mix of coconut, almonds, nuts, chia seeds.
- Add 6 Medjool Dates (remove seeds) or soaked normal dates.
- 1 tbs of coconut oil.
- Add, if you like, ¼ cup of other dried fruit like organic cranberries, apricots, etc.
- Spices to add may include cinnamon, raw cacao, nutmeg, or cacao butter to taste.
- Blend in a food processor, then roll into balls and store in the fridge or freezer.

By planning ahead and ensuring we have snacks when we are out and about can be the difference between keeping on track with your detox and intolerances or having a flair up of symptoms.

I've made it super easy to do your own 7 day detox, you will find the step by step process in the appendix at the back of the book. Enjoy the reset and recharge that comes with it.

PART III

Redefine your medicine

As Oprah Winfrey implies
"Fill up your cup and serve from your overflow"

I want you to look back to your notes on your version of happiness and health in Part I and remember what that feels like. We can often bump up against obstacles that steer us away from these positive feelings.

We are now going to really iron out any bumps or obstacles and identify where they're coming from.

In this section there are a few fact sheets and references to help define what is right for you. First we will take a look at vitamins and minerals that you might be either using up too quickly or missing in general.

Perhaps over a long period of time you haven't been eating a certain type or variety of food. You may now be that depleted that it's going to take a little bit more than just eating the food again to raise those nutrient levels in your body. This could be holding you back from everything that you require when it comes to gaining the energy levels you'd like. There are a number of different vitamin and mineral requirements needed to support those adrenal glands and build your happy hormones.

These include Zinc, B1, B6, Folate, Iron, Vitamin C, Magnesium, more B Vitamins, more Zinc, and more Vitamin C. And that is just to make adrenalin! You also need enough of these vitamins and minerals to create serotonin, which is your happy hormone that makes you feel joy and connected to other people, and melatonin that helps you sleep.

If you're missing just one of these, then you're going to have a problem with fatigue, anxiety or depression. So take a look at the vitamin and mineral table and notice any symptoms that might be occurring due to a lack of a certain nutrient.

We're going to look at the signs and symptoms and what your body is actually trying to tell you. It's not necessarily saying,

"Oh, gee, I'm tired."

Instead it might be warning you,

"I'm really rundown."

Which means I'm missing some Zinc and Vitamin C, and the chances are that you're about to come down with a cold unless you give them to your body.

Have a think about what your body is really trying to tell you, take stock of the different vitamins and minerals you may be needing and then seek out the foods that you'll find them in. Also, you may need to take a certain supplement just for a short period of time until your body gets back on track.

I'll share with you later in this section a meal planner. Although we touched on meal planning earlier, in this chapter we're really going to focus on all of the things that we've learned. I'd like you to fill out the menu plan, including some things that you found that you love and some of the things that you have found to be useful. By planning first, you avoid that concept of 'fail to plan, plan to fail.'

Then we move on to create an action plan. Your action plan is designed to be a one page wonder to glance at when you need to 'get back on track' so that you're quickly reminded of the things that are the most beneficial for you.

Sometimes your best medicine is to 'Stuff your Principles'

One of my favourite enlightened moments was meeting an aged patient when I was working in pathology in the hospital system. She gave me a golden nugget of advice when I was burnt-out, depressed and deciding whether or not to leave my full time, night shift position that I had worked so hard for after an exhausting university degree.

The conversation went something along the lines of this.

'Dear, you look terribly tired.' She said as I wheeled my trolley in, run down and disillusioned about to take her blood.

'I am.' I replied

'Well, why?'

'I'm on permanent night shift, I can't seem to catch up on my sleep and my body is doing things it hasn't before.' I felt frustrated and exhausted.

'Then why do you stay? I'm here only for a little while and I am making the most of it.' she said.

'Well, I've never quit anything in my life before. I've always done this.' I replied to her.

'Sorry to be blunt but stuff your principles.'

I was taken back by this frail old lady using such

language, but it packed a punch.
'Sometimes you just have to throw it all out, it's very nice to do the things you've always done but sometimes, for your sanity, there are just moments where you have to stuff your principles.'

This was a turning point for me. My battery was depleted. I was running on empty. At the time I was constipated, had irritable bowel syndrome, insomnia, that jet lag feeling you can never get rid of and a level of fatigue I just thought was normal.

My focus and concentration were a fraction of what I needed to do my job properly. But at the time I hadn't considered it could be any other way.

Since then I've used that lady's advice time and again. With an over saturation of health coaches, health experts and medical professionals, it's sometimes thought that we are all perfect, all of the time. That I get up at 4:30am to do my meditation, followed by an hour of yoga and resistance training, drinking my fully organic green smoothie, wearing the perfect outfit, packing the perfect lunchbox for my kids, tending to my charities in the morning before blissfully helping all my clients in the afternoon.

I am not perfect, I am human.

You are not perfect, you are human.

Running on the adrenaline of being 'perfect' all the time, is exhausting an entire generation of ambitious women and 'stuffing your principles' can be really beneficial for balancing out the rest of your neurotransmitters and happy hormones in your head.

Happy hormones and neurotransmitters

The main task of our happy hormones, or neurotransmitters, is to make us happy. But they also need balance to prevent them from turning into unhappy hormones.

Let's talk about stress to begin with. Everybody's aware of the stressors of our lives – the phone bills, the parking fines, the text messages and the time limits. All of those are psychological stressors. What most people aren't aware of is that psychological stressors cause a biochemical change in your body – the same process as if you stubbed your toe or ran a marathon, the body can't distinguish between a physical stressor and a psychological one.

We can also have emotional and mental stressors as well, which can be as simple as focusing on something for too long. For instance, watching an excessive amount of YouTube videos. All these stressors create the same biochemical response in your body.

So what is this biochemical reaction? Essentially, we're talking about the nutrients it takes to make the stress hormone, adrenalin. Adrenalin is your flight or fight hormone, which was originally used for life or death situations such as running away from a saber-toothed tiger. Now, running away from a saber-toothed tiger is a short-lived thing. We create that adrenalin to get you going, to get that thing done, and to get to the next stage.

Happy Hormones

Proteins	Zinc, B1, B6 / Stomach Acid	

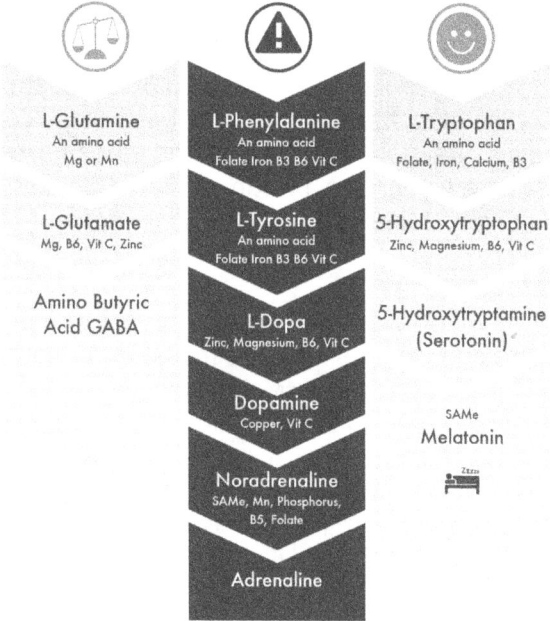

L-Glutamine An amino acid Mg or Mn	L-Phenylalanine An amino acid Folate Iron B3 B6 Vit C	L-Tryptophan An amino acid Folate, Iron, Calcium, B3
L-Glutamate Mg, B6, Vit C, Zinc	L-Tyrosine An amino acid Folate Iron B3 B6 Vit C	5-Hydroxytryptophan Zinc, Magnesium, B6, Vit C
Amino Butyric Acid GABA	L-Dopa Zinc, Magnesium, B6, Vit C	5-Hydroxytryptamine (Serotonin)
	Dopamine Copper, Vit C	SAMe Melatonin
	Noradrenaline SAMe, Mn, Phosphorus, B5, Folate	
	Adrenaline	

Unfortunately, these days we go through the process of getting something done, and then getting another thing done, and then another and another. The issue is that we're not getting downtime; we aren't letting ourselves get into a state where we're not using that adrenalin anymore.

Now to create that adrenalin it takes a whole bunch of vitamins and nutrients. The first nutrient that's needed to create any hormone in your body is protein. Proteins usually come from animal-based foods or via a combination of a grain plus a pulse or legume. As we spoke about previously, foods such as Mexican will have your kidney beans combined with rice. In Asian-based foods, we've got tofu and rice noodles. And with Mediterranean-style foods, we've got corn and legumes like chickpeas. Those grain and legume combinations form proteins in your body, the building blocks of any hormone.

The next stage is to breakdown those proteins into amino acids. You need your stomach acids to be working properly to do this. Then by adding zinc, B1, B3, and then a cascade of vitamin C, magnesium, B6 and B5, you will have successfully made adrenalin.

Now we get to dopamine. Dopamine is your aggressor hormone, your 'get stuff done' hormone. A lot of us use that every day to be, and do, and have, and feel the things that we want to feel. The issue here is that we're going to be using up a lot of nutrients to be, do, have and feel. If we don't have any downtime for our nutrients to be used in other pathways of our body, like our immune system or our reproductive system, then we're actually going to suck those nutrients away into this stress pathway.

If we're creating dopamine and adrenalin all the time – our get stuff done hormone, plus we're worried or stressed – all of those vitamins and nutrients won't be able to access our other systems. Vitamin C and zinc, for instance, are the two major nutrients that keep our skin integrity together. If you've got skin issues and you're stressed all the time, there is probably an issue with your zinc and vitamin C. And if you're putting your body under a lot of stress, then zinc and vitamin C also get used for your immune system.

When we become rundown and wonder why at the end of our stress periods, and the beginning of our holidays we get sick. We've been using up all our zinc and vitamin C to get stuff done and then our immune system goes,

"Oh, hold on, you forgot me."

Then all of a sudden; we get sick.

Magnesium, zinc, vitamin C and proteins are also used to look after your reproductive system. When you're running away from a saber-toothed tiger, like our body perceives when we use up adrenalin, you don't have time to have babies. You don't have time to be sick. So, all of it shuts down and all available nutrients head towards creating your stress hormones. Sometimes we'll even have issues with reproduction, pre-menstrual syndrome, polycystic ovarian syndrome (PCOS) and endometriosis as they have an association with our stress pathways.

After we've dealt with those stress pathways, we need to expand that picture out to include your happy hormone, serotonin, and another hormone that you may not have heard of: GABA (this one has a long crazy chemical name that we won't go into here). These are all of your neurotransmitters.

Serotonin is well-known because of the prevalence of antidepressants nowadays, and this happy hormone connects you with joy, love and feelings of connectedness with other people. We want a lot of this. The issue here is that this hormone is also created from your proteins, zinc, B1, B3, vitamin C and magnesium –

the same ingredients that create your stress hormones.

Now, serotonin is the precursor to melatonin, which helps you sleep properly. Can you see the pattern here? If you have a discrepancy between the amount of stress you have and the amount of vitamins and nutrients available, then those stress hormones will be sucking the vitamins away from your happy hormones. Because you need those happy hormones first before you can create melatonin for sleep, we start to see issues like hypersomnia (sleeping too much) or insomnia (sleeping not enough or issues falling or staying asleep).

The last one is GABA. This is your neurotransmitter that looks after your ability to have a proportionate reaction to the situations or circumstances that are occurring. One day, for instance, someone knocks over a cup of coffee next to you and it falls into your handbag or onto your suit.

"Oh, it's okay, not to worry, it was just an accident."

But the next day, the exact same thing happens and all of a sudden you're in a fluster, can't handle it, blood pressure goes up and emotions boil over.

This is a disconnection with reality. A GABA imbalance causes a disproportionate reaction, at that point in time. Again, if we can flood our system with those nutrients – zinc, vitamin C, magnesium and B vitamins – then we don't have the external and systemic issues that we might have if we're only using that stress pathway and not supporting the rest of our body with the vitamins and nutrients it needs.

A nice quick recipe for a happy hormone smoothie that contains all of the nutrients you require to feed your hormones is below:

Happy Hormone Smoothie

Banana (magnesium)
1 tsp Black strap molasses (B vitamins)
1 tbs pea, rice or hemp protein (protein)
1 cup almond milk (good fats)
¼ cup coconut milk (good fats)
1 tbsp LSA (fibre)

Blend, drink and enjoy the benefits.

Add cinnamon, vanilla or a dash of honey to taste

Happy hormone checklist

Are you experiencing...

Fluctuations in mood?

Sleep issues?

Insomnia?

Feel like you sleep all the time, and it's still not enough?

Anxiety?

Depression?

More 'flat' days than usual?

Pre Menstrual syndrome (PMS)?

Don't feel 'yourself'?

Fatigue or tiredness around 2 to 4pm in the afternoon?

Waking up exhausted?

Stressed over the smallest of things?

Discovering your medicine

This section covers the concept of everything you're eating, drinking and thinking. Your choices are either *for* your health or *against* your health.

The things you were choosing prior to reading this book could have possibly been *against* your health, and now you have the knowledge and tools to choose *for* your health.

We're doing all these beneficial things for your adrenal health and your cortisol health. By detoxing, your adrenals can reap the benefits of not having anything standing in the way. And we've being sowing the seeds to absorb all of the vitamins and minerals required through that gut lining so that our body can function optimally.

Now the other ways in which we feed our adrenals and our cortisol is through the mind, body and spirit. One tool that can really calm your mind is a gratitude journal. This exercise is also in the 7 day detox at the end of this book. It's as simple as writing down three things that you are grateful for each day. I do realise that on particularly stressful or fatigued days it can be difficult to cast your mind through the things that you may be grateful for, but please persist. I love my gratitude journal and I now do it every night before I go to bed.

One of the other tools I recommend is meditation and the practice of calming your mind. I find it best to do this in the morning. Think of it like this, you head to the shower to wash your body so why not 'wash' your mind as well? The first thing I do before I get out of bed – unless my littlest gets me up first of course – is to listen to a 15-minute meditation through an app on my smartphone.

One of my favourites is *Discovering Your Worthiness* by Lisa Nichols, which is accessible through the free app, Omvana. There is quite a selection available now, so give it a try.

So think about giving meditation a go, or find some techniques to calm your mind – even if it's just being mindful while enjoying a nice cup of tea.

Now we move on to your body. How have you enjoyed moving your body?

What are the things you're going to incorporate moving forward?

Have you noticed any symptoms or reactions when you've had dairy or sugar?

Are you more in tune with your fatigue patterns?

You should continue to develop an awareness across your whole body and incorporate any changes or improvements into your action plan.

Also take note of other things you can try that will benefit your body. Perhaps it's dry skin brushing to get your blood circulating? Or maybe there are some physical activities you would like to try?

I continue to find a multitude of different ways to move my body. I've been dancing with my kids more than I usually would, and I'm trying helicopter piloting which exercises both my body and my mind. Of course we are not all made for flying, some of my clients have tried Zumba, spin class, stand up paddle board, line dancing, pilates, and even walks at the beach or mountains.

Now we move to your spirit. What are the things you've noticed about how your spirit, your liveliness and your 'being-ness'– how you're being in the world. Really take stock on that. Revisit the section on values on page 17. Take another look at your highest priorities, your desired feelings that fire in your belly that makes you excited about the future.

What you have found works for you?

This won't be the same as everybody else, there's no right or wrong answer. Don't censor what you say, or what your lessons or insights have been. Everything that you have learned, and everything that you've done, or haven't done is exactly how it's meant to be for that moment.

Everything you've done in the past, prior to this book, has all been because you had that information at hand that gave you the exact experience you needed for that moment. That exact experience gave you the lessons so that you could move forward and change what you needed to at the time.

Vitamins and nutrients

One of the questions I always get asked is, are all vitamins the same? The short answer is no. There's a reason why some are cheap and others aren't. The contents aren't quite the same as the ones that are a little bit more expensive or found in practitioner-only brands. The difference is fivefold.

The first one is quality. The quality of your vitamins is based around the production. Where have they sourced the vitamins or minerals from? Is it a clean source? Is it a reputable source? Have they mixed it up with excipients?

Excipients are stabilisers so that the vitamins and minerals maintain their stability in the air, in travel or in heat, and the chosen excipients may be beneficial or detrimental to your body.

Quality also relates to how big the batch size is for when they create the supplement. Knowing all of this information can give you a better idea of how useful that vitamin will be when it gets into your body.

The quantity of the vitamin is equally as important. This is all about the concentration or the therapeutic dose. Just like paracetamol, aspirin or any other medications, we're going to be looking at the amounts that will be therapeutic for you to give you the effect that you're looking for. Some people can take one paracetamol and feel the effect quite quickly. Others need to take more. This is based around the quantity of paracetamol that's in that tablet. It's the same for vitamins and nutrients.

The therapeutic dose for any given day may be two for vitamin B12 or B6. It's about 50 to 100 milligrams. The problem then is to fit that into one tiny capsule. That means there's going to have to be less of something else.

This is one of the big problems with tablets or capsules that contain multiple vitamins and nutrients. If you have all of those vitamins packed in there, and at the quantity you need for it to be useful and at a high quality, then you're going to be swallowing a vitamin that's around about the size of golf ball.

There's not a lot of tablets that are around the size of a golf ball and that wouldn't be very beneficial for us to try and swallow either. Instead, manufacturers drop either quality or quantity to be able to fit them all into one tablet. This is one of the major reasons for finding out exactly which vitamins and nutrients you're lacking or that you use up quite quickly.

For example, if you were going to be using up a lot of B vitamins, then taking a B vitamin supplement with a multitude of different B's – B1, B2, B5, B6 and B12 – will be a much better option than taking your A to Z multivitamin if you're not low on the other nutrients.

The next consideration is absorption. Absorption is your ability to get the vitamin into your cells and it's based around how the vitamin or mineral is attached to another molecule that's going to absorb into a cell membrane. Some of these have to fight against each other, or need active transports, or need a whole bunch of other processes to happen so that they are absorbed. Others just soak in straightaway.

Biochemistry can be a bit of a minefield and although I am completely simplifying, generally on the bottle you are best to look for the suffix – amino acid chelate, orotate, citrate, sulfate and then last of all oxide. When you are looking at minerals this will usually help you find the more bioavailable.

The next thing to consider when you're looking at vitamins is the availability. The availability is based on how your body is functioning compared to that vitamin or mineral supplement. Availability is also based on whether or not that supplement is enterically coated. Enterically coated means there is a special coating over the tablet so it is 'easier on your stomach'. It takes a lot of effort for your body to pull a tablet apart and get to the active ingredient that's on the inside. Depending on the vitamin or mineral, you're better off having it enterically coated so it goes through the stomach and then, when it's in the bowels, completes its action. A lot of variables come into consideration when you're considering the availability of nutrients.

One of those variables is your gut and how it's functioning. Your gut is where you have the conversion of certain vitamins and minerals. Vitamin B12, for instance, converts into its active form along your gut lining. If your gut lining is not working properly, or if you've got a history of IBS or anxiety, then chances are you're not converting B12 either. The 7 day detox protocol outlines the best gut healing or find more details on page 152.

Another variable focuses on the concept of rest and digest vs fight or flight. The more stressed we get, the less likely it is that we absorb those nutrients.

The last consideration is efficacy, or how useful that vitamin has been for other people. It focuses on how efficient it is at getting those vitamins and nutrients into your body by the time you have digested it.

So quality, quantity, absorption, availability and efficacy are essential in choosing a supplement. But how do you read a supplement's ingredient panel to find these out?

Let's say I have a need for magnesium. The first word on the ingredients panel is magnesium. The second word is its form, which can hint at its absorption rate. There are multiple forms that nutrients can come in. We have orotate, which is highly absorbed, quite quickly. Diglycinate is also soaked straight into the cells, especially if you're moving. Amino acid chelate is also a fantastic form.

But there are less absorbable forms too: sulfate, oxide, carbonate and citrate. Oxide could be considered to be rust. In fact, iron oxide is rust. Therefore oxide isn't going to be the most beneficial form to have because your body is going to have to deal with the oxidation from that. Carbonate is chalk, so if you have magnesium carbonate then you're not actually absorbing much magnesium.

So, if you're looking at the back of your vitamin or mineral supplement and finding those less absorbable forms on there, you're better off finding a new supplement that's actually going to give you the therapeutic effect.

Another issue to be aware of is that Vitamin A, D, E and K are all fat-soluble vitamins, which means you need fat available to soak them up. Due to this, it's important that you purchase these vitamins in oil forms otherwise they will not be absorbed.

The next thing that you'll notice on the ingredients panel is the quantity. For instance, the registered amount for zinc is around 25 milligrams, which is going to make you feel like you're bursting with energy. It's also going to give you healthy immunity, skin, happy hormones and a host of other things that it's used for. Zinc also has a role in holding your mucous membrane integrity together. If you have a normal level of zinc, then you will want the therapeutic dose. If you take more than 25 milligrams you might experience stomach irritation and feel a bit nauseous. If you have less than that therapeutic dose then you're not really going to get the effect of the zinc.

Side note: the therapeutic amount of magnesium for most conditions like restless legs, cramping in your legs or feet, headaches, not being able to rebound after exercise, sleeplessness and other tense or jerky issues with your muscles is about 300 milligrams.

Another aspect we need to consider is competition. The competition concept is based around the idea that your cells have a whole bunch of locks and multiple keys can open those locks. For example, the key for iron can open a multitude of locks. But those locks also use the same key for zinc. The problem is if you've got two keys and one lock, there's going to be competition for which one is going to get into the cell. Whenever you find a supplement that has both iron and zinc in there, depending on your levels, you're not going to get one of them.

This can be quite difficult for people who have anemia as well as zinc issues, and it's important that they take their iron and zinc at different times of the day. Magnesium and calcium have a similar competitive issue, but you also need enough magnesium for calcium to be absorbed, and enough calcium for magnesium to be absorbed.

Despite all the discussions on supplements, do not forget vitamins and minerals are available in your foods too! If you keep all of your vitamins and mineral levels up and your stressors low, then you should be able to get them through your food with perhaps a couple of top-ups during the year. Your body can remain in balance and look after itself given the right environment.

Take note that vitamins and minerals in foods can also be impacted by heat or light. Some of those major vitamins and minerals are zinc and B vitamins. Up to 90% of B vitamins are lost through cooking and through exposure to light. Some of the fruits and vegetables that we're having from the supermarkets have been exposed to UV light during transportation to the supermarket, and then sit overnight under the fluorescent lights. Some of those vitamins and minerals are really minimised by the time you have a bite of that apple or that carrot.

Beta-carotene is one of those affected by light as well. Interestingly, it's one of the reasons that root vegetables grow underground. This is another reason why it is always best to purchase your fruits and vegetables from your local markets.

Vitamins and nutrients fact sheet

Vitamins	Food Sources
B1 (twitches, tingly hands/feet)	Asparagus, Brewer's yeast, Liver, Red Meat (60% is lost in cooking)
B2 (eyes, skin, migraines)	Eggs, Dairy, Almond, Asparagus, Sprouts, broccoli, currants, avocado, wholegrains (10% lost in cooking)
B3 (Tummy problems, metabolism, nervous system)	Fish, beef, legumes, chicken, sunflower seeds, almond, yeast (stable in heat)
B5 (Adrenal stress, anxiety, mood)	Wholegrains, avocado, blue cheese, organ meat, mushrooms, sweet potato, wholegrains, green veg, eggs (50% lost when milled or canned)
B6 (Dream recall, anxiety, mood)	Yeast, eggs, organ meat, nuts/seeds, fish, banana, carrot (unstable in light)
B12 (Energy, mood)	Eggs, Organ Meat, synthesized by bacteria, sardines, salmon, oysters, Swiss cheese (between 10-90% lost in cooking)
Vitamin C (Healing, skin)	Berries, Broccoli, Oranges, Citrus, brussel sprouts, pineapple, parsley (unstable to heat and light)

Vitamins	Food Sources
Calcium (Cramps or bone issues)	Almond, Tofu, Broccoli, Buckwheat, egg yolk, sardines, green leafy veg
Folate (Mood issues)	Greens, lentils, barley
Vitamin D (hormone disregulation, bone materials)	Eggs, fish liver oils, butter, milk, sprouted seeds
Vitamin K (trouble clotting)	Gut bacteria, Greens, Kelp, liver, soy
Magnesium (Used in 325 different pathways, mood, muscles, stress, sleep)	Banana, Walnut, Almond, Cashews, Figs, Eggs, cocoa, wholegrains
Zinc (hair, teeth, skin, nails, immunity, healing)	Oysters, Mussels, Seafood, Capsicum, yeast
Selenium (thyroid, nails)	Brazil nuts, yeast, onion, fish, garlic
Iodine (thyroid)	Kelp, Seaweed
Iron (Fatigue, easy bruising, pallor)	Red Meat, Kangaroo, chicken, pumpkin seeds, pine nuts, green leafy, apricots
Protein (Hair, skin, nails, hormones)	Turkey, Kangaroo, Eggs, Combined grain plus pulse, Chicken, Fish
Essential Fatty Acids (brain, mood, thinking, skin)	Fish, Avocado, Nuts, Seeds

Symptoms fact sheet

Vitamins and herbs you may like to consider (of course check with your health practitioner to see if it is right for you)

Symptom	Vitamin/Herb
Fatigue	B12, Iron, B5, B6, Ginseng
Headache	Mg, B12, B2, Feverfew
Mood swings, emotional	Essential fatty acids, B's, Zinc, Withania
Nausea/Bloating/Flatulence	Probiotics, B12, Fennel, Peppermint, Chamomile
Cold/Flu coming on	Vit C, Zinc, Echinacea, Astragalus
Can't concentrate	B12, Brahmi, Ginkgo
Bruise easily	Iron, Butchers broom
Nails (Ridges or white flecks)	Protein and Zinc, Horsetail
Skin (Dry, Rashes)	Zinc , Vit C, Vitamin A, Chickweed
Skin (Pallor)	Iron, B12, Folate, Nettle
Hair	Protein, Horsetail
Cramps legs and feet	Mg, Calcium, Cramp bark
Sleep issues	Mg, Chamomile, Hops, Kava, Passionflower
No night vision	Vitamin A, Bilberry
Painful tongue	B5, B6, B12, Calendula
Bleeding gums	B3, Vit C, Golden Seal
Small cuts around mouth (Angular stomatitis)	B2, Zinc, Vitamin C, Thyme
Bone pain	Vit C, Vit D, Calcium, Magnesium, Arnica

Plants as medicine

Often we don't think of herbs and how they can be used to help solve our ailments. We're so used to having a drug culture where we're prescribed lab-created drugs that have the desired effect.

Herbs, however, are alive. Different species grow in certain areas of the world, and are picked and processed where they thrive. And depending on the herb, different parts of the plant are used. For instance, Echinacea flower tops are used – rather than the whole plant – which is useful as you're able to just chop the tops off. This gives the plant the opportunity to grow back before using the flowers again.

The Gingko tree is similar. It is left to grow as big as it possibly can and when it sheds its leaves each season, these are harvested without the rest of the tree being touched.

However some of our root herbs need to grow up to thirteen years to gain their full therapeutic effect, so their constituents are the most useful.

Turmeric, for instance, takes three years to grow for the tuber to create all the curcumin needed. So when you pick turmeric, you can't just take the roots – you're digging up the entire herb, harvesting the roots, and then the whole process has to start again.

The cost of some of those herbs can be expensive because of the way in which they're grown and where they're actually sourced. Some herbs are becoming extinct, just like animals on the planet. They only grow in certain areas. Then when they're picked (wild crafted), or completely taken out of their natural environment, there aren't many left.

So, when you're considering the types of herbs that you need for your cold or flu for instance, find out where they come from or how abundant they're growing. This is helpful to know as rare or less abundant herbs may be adulterated or swapped with another herb before it gets into your bottle. This can often happen with herbs where the root is used, but happens less often if the leaves, tops, berries or bark is used as they can be harvested without taking the whole plant.

Mental health

There was a time my husband was worried about my mental health. One Sunday afternoon, he told me in no uncertain terms to take a walk around the block. For a few months I had been a little jealous that he had found his sport – mountain bike riding.

He would go out every Saturday on his two thousand dollar mountain bike and come back an hour later, much to my disgust. He would come back vibrant, not a care in the world, but I would be cranky, unable to let go of the challenge of balancing kids and business.

If I wasn't at work, I was looking after the kids and if I wasn't looking after the kids, I was at work.

There was nothing in between.

A couple of months prior, a good friend had asked me to write down five things I had always wanted to try or that I'd always loved. In the midst of my work/home blur, I was disappointed to find that I had no idea what those things were. It took me a couple of weeks to write a list and a couple more to actually do something about them.

My task was simple, I just had to ring and find out when it was on.

The problem I found was that I already had it in my head that it would clash with the children's activities, or that it was going to cost more than I thought it would. The reality was that I made those assumptions without having called first.

I finally rang the rock climbing centre, the first on the list. I needed a partner to go and it was going to cost $20. Even though I had bought my son $200 soccer boots only weeks before, somehow in my mind I was having a hard time justifying a $20 lesson for myself.

I finally went, climbed up that wall, got to the top and… never wanted to do it again.

But since I had the momentum going, it didn't take as much effort to call the next activity on the list, dance classes. The times just didn't line up with our family, so I went to the next on the list – roller derby.

Again I had it in my head that it was going to cost $495 for skates and pads and that it would clash with our family duties. It took until that fateful Sunday after Murray sternly told me to go for a walk, to actually go.

I sat in the car outside for a little while, fuming that he had told me to 'get some fresh air,' mumbling under my breath that he had hours of fresh air every Saturday, so how dare he tell me to!

Then I realised it was about the time that roller derby was on and I thought I may as well go and watch. When I got there I discovered it cost $5 to hire skates and for the next two hours I couldn't think about my business, my husband, my family, my fuming. All I could think about was not falling on my bum and putting one foot in front of the other.

I came back home that afternoon an entirely different person. I could not have fathomed the transformation in my mood, energy, focus and self-esteem. I continued to do roller derby for another eighteen months and loved it. I had something new to talk to my kids about, my husband looked at me differently and I had a whole new way of viewing myself.

Now I am sure I could've taken some pharmaceutical medication to ease the anxiety and depressive symptoms I was having but by keeping my mind open and re-defining my medicine I was able to get through a pretty dark patch in my life.

Find your bliss

The monks know all about the mind and spirit side of things. Some amazing studies have been done on monks to register cortisol as well as different parts of the brain that deal with stress, resilience and energy levels, comparing them in a meditative and non-meditative state. Cortisol is one of the most significant of those to be tested. It's amazing the ability they have to just switch off, to really tune in or tune out.

So how can we decrease cortisol in our daily lives, since we have numerous things on a day-to-day basis that throw our cortisol here, there and everywhere? There are a number of different activities we can choose to do – one of them is reading books. Books can be used to escape or elevate. Now, escapism is pretty much avoidance but it can be useful to decrease your cortisol. Whereas the books that are going to elevate your spirit, or inspire you, or drive you to a place of joy, they're more likely to be having the long-term effects that we want to see when it comes to being energised and stress free.

The next one we can integrate into our daily lives is meditation. We've already spoken about meditation and hopefully by now you've had a chance to try it out for yourself and find out which type you like. It can really re-regulate that cortisol and set you up for more resilience in the future.

Other ways we can have bliss in our daily lives is travel. Travel takes us out of our current state, changes the environment in which we're in and it changes the way that we perceive our environment as well.

Learning something new is another good tool to bring down your cortisol. Initially there is an increase in cortisol because you're feeling out of your comfort zone. But, in the long run, the science has shown that learning something new can actually set up that resilient system, it can set you up for bouncing back from anything else that's new or changes.

The next one is getting out in nature. It only needs to be fifteen minutes for it to be incredibly beneficial for energy, decreasing stress and creating more resilience. It could even be fifteen minutes in the park at lunchtime, heading down to the beach, spending time in your garden or going for a bushwalk during the weekend. These all bring down your cortisol.

Another way to find your bliss is through your relationships, first with yourself and with the significant others in your life. Professor Waring a lecturer in Psychology at the University of Newcastle was the keynote speaker at a conference on Human Resources. He mentioned research on couples, their mental attitude and the rate of breakups. He discovered five main points that were not only beneficial for mental health in the long run, but also for the longevity of relationships.

The first point is taking time out. The magic number is around four hours per week doing something you enjoy that doesn't have to do with work and doesn't have to do with home. You need to focus on feeding that part of you that might have been given over to somebody else or something else in your life.

The next point is positive anticipation – having something that you can look forward to. For most people this is usually their next holiday or travel experience. But it can also be something that you're doing next week. It's a great idea to have something that you look forward to each week – such as a class to learn something new – so that you can feel positive anticipation on a regular basis.

The third point he found common for good relationships was having a *good mate*, somebody you can talk to, somebody that you can lean on that, again, it doesn't have to do with work, and it doesn't have to do with home.

The fourth one is belonging to a group outside of your home or outside of your profession, a group where you can get a different perspective on the world, or a different perspective to what's going on in your life. Belonging to a group of likeminded individuals also satisfies a need that we have, a primal urge for having a tribe.

The last point is regularly reviewing your life. This review usually happens when the year is starting to end, but it's good to do this regularly. We should review what's been going on for us and what changes have been made in our lives.

All of these points revolve around finding things that move you closer to bliss and joy. How do you know what you would like to do if you've never stopped to take the time to find out? The number one question I ask most of my female clients is,

"*If we had you doing something that you enjoy, what would that look like?*"

The number one response I get back is,

"*I wouldn't even know where to start. I don't know what*

that is."

So, just start trying things. Pick up a book to read. Or listen to an audiobook, which can be downloaded onto an electronic device like a smart phone. They're cheaper than a real book and you can listen to them wherever you are – even when doing the housework or in the car.

Choose some form of movement that you enjoy. It doesn't have to be boot camp, or flogging it out at the gym – though if you do enjoy those things, go right ahead. But it could also be dance or rock climbing. Find some form of movement and try different things.

Other options are finding a class. Pick something that you're interested in learning how to do and contact the organiser. Just be conscious of not putting up roadblocks for yourself by creating answers to questions you haven't even asked yet – don't assume that activities are going to be too expensive, if they're going to be on the right day, or they won't fit in with your family or lifestyle. Find a class, or something that you're interested in, and check it out.

And if you haven't already booked a holiday, activity or event that you have positive anticipation around, then it's time to start planning one. It could be as simple as organising a night away. Having that positive anticipation of something to look forward to gives you that light at the end of the tunnel on the days where things start to get a bit too much.

Creating an action plan

So, for example, you may have found that it's easy for you to consume more fruits and vegetables in the form of smoothies or juices. Therefore you would place those on your Eat More list. You also may have noticed that dairy or gluten are not the best choices for you, so you would pop those on your Eat Less list to be reminded of this?

The next section focuses on your herbs and vitamins. After you've looked through the vitamin and mineral list and checked out which symptoms might apply to you, jot these down on your action plan. This can help to remind you to take any supplements, or perhaps consume more foods with these nutrients in them.

The area below that is about finding something that you enjoy doing as physical movement. I don't like using the word 'exercise' because most people have a negative connotation around that. But moving every day is highly important, even if it's just going for a walk around the block or getting out in nature. Choose something fun and make sure to keep it achievable.

The final area focuses on seeking help. This is where you jot down anything that you have noticed your body's been telling you. Perhaps it needs a massage, maybe your arches in your feet need addressing, maybe you need to check in with your dentist to see how your teeth are going, or maybe you need to see your local naturopath.

Writing these things down often means that they you will get them done and not ignored.

Also add to your action plan any extra things that you have wanted to try or goals that you want to reach. By writing it down and putting your plan into practice it is going to benefit your adrenal glands, your stress and your energy levels.

ACTION PLAN

AIM: Freedom from fatigue

Eat More	Eat Less

Herbs and Vitamins

Physical Movement

Seeking help	

So, to recap…

Choose one to start following your bliss and bring your stress hormones down.

1. Take time out, 1 - 4 hours a week doing something that you enjoy.

2. Positive Anticipation - have something to look forward to.

3. Find a good mate to share experiences with.

4. Join a group / activity that lights you up.

5. Review your life regularly.

PART IV

Recharge

Recharging from adrenal fatigue needs to be treated like traffic lights.

There needs to be a period of time (usually around 6 weeks) that you have a red light. You stop doing things that exhaust you or stress you physically, emotionally or mentally. This may be a break from exercise, it's not working anyway when your body is under stress. You may need to delegate jobs so you don't have everything on your plate, or it could be learning to say 'No' to things that zap your energy. Whatever it is, you literally have to stop and pull back before you can leap forward.

If you jump ahead too soon, you will only end up more tired, injured or sick.

The next phase of recharging is the yellow/amber light. Like a traffic light, sometimes you can get away with putting your foot down and accelerating through and other times you get caught out and you would be better off just stopping. This phase is generally around 6 weeks as well. This is the time you can re-introduce gentle non-competitive movement like yoga, pilates, tai chi or walking. It is also a time to ensure you have vitamin and herbal support for adapting to life at a faster pace.

But it is still important to delegate and say 'No' when you need to so you don't wear yourself out. If you move too quickly from the red light to green light, you can over-rev your engine and burn-out again. It is a fine line and it's best to check in with how your body feels, not what your mind thinks.

The final phase is green light, this comes when you are no longer feeling fatigued in the afternoons and you are more alert and energised the majority of your mornings.

If you've taken action on the previous chapters, like hundreds of my clients, chances are that you have doubled your energy and halved your stress.

If you practice the things that work for you from this book over a period of three to six months, your level of vitality will have you sparkling.

But what then?

And what about the ups and downs of life?

Just like the battery in our digital devices, depending on how we use them, we can get depleted. If you are teetering on the cusp of the dreaded 20% battery life and the red light is on, then it's not long before you either have to shut down or find a way to recharge.

There are times in life where we have every App open, we are juggling so many projects, so many goals. Our battery life is much more limited at these points in time. We become run down so much quicker. The crucial thing going forward is to know what's your 'red light' or your warning signals. How do you recognise when you are at the dreaded 20% mark?

What are your optimal conditions to recharge?

Throughout this book you have had the chance to explore what works for you.

Are you doing things in alignment with your values on page 17?

Do you need a reset with a detox on page 67?

Are you potentially missing some nutrients and need a boost from page 131?

Is it more water you require - see page 85

Do you need some extra sleep on page 90

Maybe it's time out to really focus on your bliss on page 139.

If you find yourself run down again, bring back those practices and remedies that help you be the best version of you.

My vision

I dream of a place where the women who are changing the world have all their medicine on hand to embody the vitality needed to create the impact that we are born to make. I envisage a connection between the entrepreneurial mind and spirit, that is fed and nourished by not only vision and drive but revitalised cells that house the foundations of creating the platform for their message to get out into the world.

Final checklist

1. Remember you have a body

2. Remember who you are
   - Your values
   - Feelings
   - Natural talents

3. Remove obstacles
   - Detox
   - Heal your gut
   - Food intolerances
   - Wellness Wheel

4. Redefine your medicine
   - Vitamin and mineral optimisation
   - Find and follow your bliss

5. Recharge – Red light, orange light, green light

7 Day Detox Protocol

(Originally co-authored with Amanda Daley www.amandajdaley.com)

So, we've read about all the various Toxins we put into our body and the benefits of removing them, including how essential it is to balance our hormones and eliminating anything standing in the way of abundant energy.

I know that you are crazy busy, and that's why I've made this action plan as simple as possible for maximum results. I've pulled everything you need into one easy to follow plan. Now all you need to do is COMMIT and follow along.

Staying committed is the key - even if an unexpected deadline drops in your lap or some brain wave of an idea pops up that you want to take action on right now. The thing is, these things will ALWAYS get in the way, that's life - but you are in control and choosing to put yourself first will be irreplaceable.

So, if life gets in your way, keep some perspective - it's just 7 days and if you follow the plan, your body will LOVE you for it!!

What's going to happen?

What you might experience

Everyone experiences detox differently. Initially, in the first two days or so, you may experience symptoms of fatigue, nausea, or headaches as toxins leave your body. This is usually experienced as withdrawal from sugar or caffeine.

It may also be 'die-off' which is the process of bad bacteria dying in the digestive tract. Again, this is a passing thing. If it's too uncomfortable, stop immediately. This is nothing to worry about - keep up the two litres of water a day, juice and follow the program and the symptoms will pass.

By the end of seven days you may also experience any of the following:

- Increased Energy

- Reduced Bloating

- Eliminated Sugar Cravings

- Deeper Sleep

- Weight Loss

- Easier to deal with stress

Pre-tox

A pre-tox day gives you an opportunity to get what you need, slow down on things you don't and get in the mindset for a kick-start.

The day before your detox it is ideal to gradually eliminate dairy, sugar, processed food, caffeine, alcohol, bread, pasta, and any other refined, packaged, canned or preserved products from your diet.

The idea is to start to make space for the cleansing process, so it is an easier transition on your body - with less side effects as a result.

Be 100% prepared

Being prepared is THE 'make or break' action to take when starting your detox.

Willpower alone will not get you through a busy afternoon at work; you know the time - when your energy slumps around 3pm and the fundraiser chocolates are right in front of you at that exact weak moment.

Hiccups WILL happen. So will the emergency with the kids or that last minute job you didn't think you would have to do until Monday.

External situations are out of your control, but you can have your food prepared as a fall back, no matter what pops up. If you can take an hour for lunch, awesome - but if it doesn't happen, then your meal is already to go and you can stop for ten minutes to relax and be present as you feed yourself with nutrients.

Preparation is the key to success when it comes to a detox. If you have the opportunity to shop for the shopping list items and prepare three meals in advance it will allow things to run much more smoothly.

So, to fully prepare yourself, your time and your body I recommend buying everything you need in advance, get your snacks ready by pre-chopping cucumber, celery and carrot sticks and store in a glass container with a little water and the lid tight (these should be fresh for 3 days in the fridge).

Pre-pack nuts, no more than twenty for snacking.

Make a batch of broccoli or pumpkin soup and keep in fridge (or freezer).

Roast root vegetables – carrot, sweet potato, pumpkin, beetroot and put in airtight container in the fridge.

Make a big fruit salad for breakfast, or have bananas and rice bran ready to go.

On the menu

VEGGIES

Choose from a wide variety of vegetables in season. The detox moves from 100% greens on the first day to rainbow colours during the week, so stock up on plenty of green leafy vegetables and varieties of 5 other colours.

FRUIT

Fruit can be eaten first thing each day in a smoothie or fruit salad and one more time during the day as a snack. Don't forget avocado and tomato are fruit too. Half an avocado a day is fantastic for good fat and looking after your glucose.

HERBS AND SPICES

Use as many herbs and spices as you like to taste, coriander and parsley are particularly useful in detox, as is turmeric.

WHOLEGRAINS

These are introduced after day 1 and 2 and it's recommended that you stick to gluten-free whole grains. Go for quinoa, buckwheat, linseed/sunflower and almond meal, brown or basmati rice, millet and amaranth.

BEANS AND LEGUMES

Eat a variety of adzuki, cannellini, lima, kidney, navy and black beans along with chickpeas and lentils. Canned will do if you don't have the time to soak.

SEAFOOD

Seafood is introduced halfway through the week. Where possible buy local fish. If buying tinned, look for one in water or olive oil.

MEAT- only if you eat it (eggs if possible)

Limited amounts of turkey, chicken, lamb, and beef can be slowly introduced after the first couple of days of the detox. Always shop for grass-fed meat, ideally organic.

NUTS and SEEDS

All nuts and seeds are allowed on the detox, except peanuts, which can grow a type of mould. Nuts are a great source of good fat.

OILS

Use coconut oil, olive oil, flaxseed oil, or sesame oil as dressings or to lightly cook with.

Shopping list

- Filtered water or jug

- A variety of vegetables, with an emphasis on leafy greens

- Fruit

- Herbs and spices

- Apple Cider Vinegar

- Nuts and seeds

- Oils

- Beans and legumes

- Local fish

- Organic, grass-fed chicken, lamb or beef

- Organic herbal teas

- Gluten-free grains (Brown or basmati rice, quinoa, millet, amaranth)

Off the menu

I'm a big believer in crowding out the not-ideal foods with good stuff but there are a few items that are strictly off the menu.

Avoid **gluten, dairy, refined sugar, alcohol, caffeine, processed food (anything in a tin or package), vinegar (except Apple Cider Vinegar), margarine and takeaways.**

Supplement Support

Try the following supplements for extra support if required:

St Mary's Thistle - For your liver

Vitamin B - if energy is a problem

Vitamin C - if immunity or inflammation is a problem

Probiotic - if IBS or bloating is a problem

Magnesium - if cramps, relaxing or headaches are a problem

Glutamine - if hormones and tummy is an issue

DAY ONE – ACTIONS

Today's Intention: I choose to be happy

Manifest your mood with a clear intention

The very first thing to do when you wake up each day is *choose* how you would like this day of your life to be. Read today's intention, if you can, say it out loud as though it is already true. Really feel the feeling of it already being true and intend that your day will continue to feel that way. *Choosing* how we start our day aligns our values and desires of exactly what we intend to attract. Just try it, even if it feels a little out of your norm, it's only 7 days, you never know what will happen.

CLEAN EATING

Greens are good!

Green vegetables are the least likely food to appear in modern diets. Make friends with your greens by learning to cook and eat greens.

Nutritionally, greens are very high in folate, calcium, magnesium, iron, potassium, phosphorous, zinc and vitamins A, C, E and K. They are full of fibre, chlorophyll and many other micronutrients and phytochemicals. Whenever possible, choose organic. But if budget is an issue, eating non-organic greens is much better than not eating any greens at all!

CHILL PILL
Re-affirm your values and vision

20 minutes before bed take out your values and definition of health and happiness 23. See what comes up, are they still sitting well with you? Do they need editing? Maybe you have thought up a new word. Try to cultivate that feeling of when you were the most YOU, you have ever been. Hold it as long as you can.

Prepare for the week ahead

Minimise stress by getting all the preparation out of the way. Knowing that your food is all ready to go will stop anxiety building around 'getting it right' while detoxing and allow you to relax. All you have to do is prepare ahead and then follow along step by step each day.

DAY ONE - PLAN

ON RISING
Warm water with dash of lemon juice or 1 tsp Apple
Cider Vinegar in 100 ml Water

BREAKFAST
DETOX SMOOTHIE: Mix 1 banana (or preferred fruit or
veg), 1 cup of either apple, prune or coconut juice, 1 cup
water, 1 tbsp Rice Bran or Chia or Linseed/Sunflower
and Almond meal (LSA)

LUNCH
Green salad, roast or steamed green vegetables, lemon
juice as dressing

DINNER
Steamed or roasted green veggies OR Green Soup

SNACKS (OPTIONAL)
Celery, capsicum or cucumber sticks if needed

BEFORE BED
1 cup apple, coconut water or prune juice, 1 cup water,
1 tbsp Rice Bran/LSA

WATER
2 litres throughout the day

EXERCISE
20 min walk in nature

DAY TWO – ACTIONS

Today's Intention: I live a colourful life full of love

Cleanse your mind just like your body

Spend 10 minutes each morning clearing your mind and opening your heart before you start the day. Or just sit quietly and focus on your breathing for a few minutes each morning.

CLEAN EATING

Eat rainbow foods: Now that you have be-friended green vegetables it's time to add in some of their colourful relatives. While it's important to still have at least half a plate of green vegetables, you can start to add a few different colours to the mix.

Look for Red (tomato, pepper, chilli, radish, beetroot), Orange (pumpkin, sweet potato, kumara, carrot), Purple (eggplant, purple cabbage, purple carrot), Yellow (corn, yellow squash, ginger, turmeric), White (parsnips, cauliflower, onion, garlic) – and of course all the fruits too.

CHILL PILL
Journaling

30 minutes before bed, journal. Start the journal with an intention for your next 3 weeks (that is how long it takes to create a habit) - what do you intend to gain as a result of bringing your body, mind and spirit back into balance?

Follow this with writing three things you are grateful for today. Then fill the page with whatever is on your mind.

"I found today hard because..."

"I'm nervous about finishing my project on time..." etc.

Anything that comes to mind, get it down on paper and out of your mind, so that your mind is a blank canvas - allowing your body to sleep much deeper - healing and repairing every cell as we detox.

DAY TWO - PLAN

ON RISING
Meditation or simply focussing on the breath for a few minutes

Warm water with dash of lemon juice OR Apple cider vinegar, 1 tsp in 100 ml of water

BREAKFAST
DETOX SMOOTHIE: Mix 1 banana (or preferred fruit), 1 cup preferred juice or non dairy milk, 1 cup water, 1 tbsp Rice Bran or Chia or LSA - blender

LUNCH
Green salad, roast or steamed green vegetables, lemon juice as dressing

DINNER
Steamed or roasted veggies OR Soup

SNACKS (OPTIONAL)
Celery, carrot, cucumber or capsicum sticks or nuts if needed

BEFORE BED
1 cup apple, coconut water or prune juice, 1 to 2 cup water, 1 tbsp Rice Bran/LSA

WATER
2 litres throughout the day

EXERCISE
20 min walk or stretching

DAY THREE - ACTIONS

Today's Intention: I honour my body's highs and lows.

Action Step: Dry skin brushing

Your lymphatic system is a waste disposal chute for toxins. Unlike the blood, which has the heart to pump it around the body, the lymph has no pump of its own and needs a bit of a helping hand.

Gentle exercise gets the lymph flowing as does dry body brushing because it sits just between the skin and the muscles. Pick up a natural bristle brush from your local health food store and brush gently over your skin in short strokes - always towards the heart. Doing this on dry skin before your morning shower is ideal, it is not as affective when you are already in the shower, as the hot water will be flowing your lymph already.

CLEAN EATING

Beans and legumes: Beans and legumes are a wonderful way to add high-quality, plant-based protein to your diet. They are high in iron, B vitamins, and fibre, and there are a wide variety of them. Economical and easy to cook, beans and legumes bulk up a plant based meal to keep you healthy but full.

You can try adzuki, cannellini, lima, kidney, navy and black beans along with chickpeas and lentils.

These also make amazing dips when blended with a little olive oil and dash of tahini. Canned is fine, just make sure they are rinsed thoroughly before use.

Legumes are a debatable topic in some lifestyle choices so it is good to keep in mind they can be difficult to breakdown in some tummies, so be mindful about if the react with you.

CHILL PILL

In bed by 10pm

It is essential for recovery of adrenals to be in bed before 10pm to allow your body to complete its rejuvenation during the night. The adrenal glands pump cortisol at its highest in the morning, and to train the cortisol, it is best to be asleep between 9:30 - 10pm, when cortisol should be at its lowest. If you miss this precious window for falling asleep, the adrenals will get a second wind adding fuel to the fire of burnout.

DAY THREE - PLAN

ON RISING
MEDITATION OR Body brush before shower

Lemon juice in water or ACV in water

BREAKFAST
Fruit salad plus 1 cup preferred juice or Smoothie, 1 cup water, 1 tbs Rice Bran or Chia or LSA

Juice/Smoothie option- Coconut water, banana, kiwi, berries

LUNCH
Fresh salad or steamed vegetables, lemon juice, olive oil and herbs / spices as dressing
Mixture of green and coloured veggies and include ½ cup of legumes if you would like

DINNER
Steamed or roasted mixed veggies with herbs and spices - Can include beans and lentils – Mexican or Middle Eastern dishes would be ideal

SNACKS (OPTIONAL)
Celery, carrot, capsicum or cucumber sticks if needed
Add homemade hummus or tahini dip

BEFORE BED
1/2 cup apple or prune juice, 1/2 cup water, 1 tbsp Rice Bran/Chia/LSA

WATER
2 litres throughout the day

EXERCISE
Try some yoga, 20 minutes, try to release any tension that has emerged throughout the day

DAY FOUR - ACTIONS

Today's Intention: It is safe to put me first.

Action Step: Walk a different way to work

Get your creative juices flowing and build new neural pathways. Exposing ourselves to new environments can trigger senses, which are otherwise dormant, and as you detox, your body will improve its senses all round - making these mini adventures even more powerful.

You might be surprised at what you find in your own neighbourhood! Breaking your routine early in the day helps you to start the day on a positive note, stopping feelings of being 'stuck in a rut' in their tracks.

CLEAN EATING

Variety is the spice of life: Herbs and spices not only give instant flavour to any meal but they are jam packed with healing properties too. Experiment with different flavours while detoxing, and then continue to use them like 'medicine.'

Cayenne/Chilli: Boosts metabolism and reduces congestion

Cinnamon: Powerful blood sugar balancer

Turmeric: Fights cancer, reduces inflammation and balances hormones

Nutmeg: Antibacterial helps improve memory and reduces depression

Coriander: Reduces anxiety and helps with digestion

Garlic: Anti-bacterial and anti-fungal plus a powerful anti-oxidant

Ginger: Improves digestion and wards off nausea

Mustard: Breaks up congestions and improves circulation

Rosemary: Great for memory and heart

CHILL PILL
Feel your emotions

As your body starts to release toxins, you will start to be able to feel your emotions clearer than before. This is a good thing, although at first it can be a new experience.

Emotions (or the chemicals that make them) get trapped in our cells, science calls this 'cellular memory' and so with the release of toxins from our bodies emotions can also come up to be released. The most common emotion to arise during a detox is Anger as it resides in the liver. Whatever new emotions you may feel during your detox, don't panic, but rather allow yourself to actually feel them. An emotion fully felt only really lasts 30 seconds and then it is released from the cell. Give it a go!

Yell into a cushion, stomp your feet, cry over a movie, or go for a run to feel the emotions fully and then feel the relaxation flood into your body as it is freed up.

DAY FOUR – PLAN

BREAKFAST
Meditation or stretch

Lemon water or ACV water

Fruit Salad – 1 cup preferred juice, 1 cup water, 1 tbsp
Rice Bran or chia seeds or LSA. Juice option-
Orange/Carrot/Celery/Mint

LUNCH
Fresh salad, roasted or steamed vegetables, lemon
juice, olive oil and herbs/ spices as dressing. You can
add beans or Tuna/Salmon if you choose.

DINNER
Steamed mixed veggies with herbs and spices – include
beans and lentils

You can include fish – Fresh local Fish or Salmon

SNACKS (OPTIONAL)
Celery, capsicum or cucumber sticks or nuts if needed
Carrot sticks with homemade hummus or tahini dip

BEFORE BED
1 cup apple or prune juice, 1 cup water, 1 tbsp Rice
Bran/LSA

WATER
2 litres throughout the day

EXERCISE
20 min walk or yoga

JOURNAL before bed

DAY FIVE – ACTIONS

TAKE CARE of YOU

Today's Intention: I love and appreciate every cell in my body

Alternate Nostril Breathing

Alternate nostril breathing is an Ayurvedic tradition often used in yoga, it will help you to de-stress AND lose weight! This breathing technique helps to lower your cortisol - one of your fight or flight chemicals that gets released into the body when stress arises.

Sit comfortably with your spine erect and shoulders relaxed. Keep a gentle smile on your face.

Place the tip of the index finger and middle finger of the right hand in between the eyebrows, the ring finger and little finger on the left nostril, and the thumb on the right nostril. We will use the ring finger and little finger to open or close the left nostril and thumb for the right nostril.

Press your thumb down on the right nostril and breathe out gently through the left nostril.

Now breathe in from the left nostril and then press the left nostril gently with the ring finger and little finger. Removing the right thumb from the right nostril, breathe out from the right.

Breathe in from the right nostril and exhale from the left. You have now completed one round.

Continue inhaling and exhaling from alternate nostrils.

Complete nine such rounds by alternately breathing through each nostril.

After every exhalation, remember to breathe in from the same nostril from which you exhaled. Keep your eyes closed throughout and continue taking long, deep, smooth breaths without any force or effort.

Once your internal chemistry is rebalanced, and functioning normally again, you will feel calmer and make decisions from a much more rational place.

You will also find that your body will switch to using sugar to give you energy – so it won't get stored as fat.

CLEAN EATING

Grains: Whole grains have been a central element of the human diet since early civilization. Humans ceased being hunter-gatherers and settled down into farming communities when they were able to cultivate grain crops. People living in these communities—on all continents—had lean, strong bodies and very few people were overweight. While grains can be associated with carbohydrates, which can make people run for the hills in fear of weight gain, the whole variety (think brown rice not white) are nutritional powerhouses. It can be useful to soak your grains before cooking them (ideally overnight) to break down the indigestible 'phytic acid' coating.

Whole grains balance our blood sugar and stabilise our hormones, contain essential enzymes, iron, dietary fibre, vitamin E and B-complex vitamins. Because the body absorbs grains slowly, they provide sustained and high-quality energy

For the duration of the detox I encourage you to only eat Gluten Free grains. These include: Basmati rice, brown rice, buckwheat, millet, amaranth and quinoa.

CHILL PILL
Eat Lunch in Nature

When the body is in a stressed state it literally cannot digest food properly – you can either have "fight or flight" or "rest and digest" - meaning that all those healthy greens could be passing straight through you without you absorbing their wonderful benefits. In the coming weeks, try and step outside your office to eat your lunch in nature each day. Either explore the local food court for a healthy salad, or ideally, bring a pre-prepared meal and find a local park to sit in and eat in a relaxed manner. If there really is nowhere outside the office to eat (are you really sure that's the case?) then pop out for a walk around the block before or after lunch to help your system relax and get your daily dose of Vitamin D.

DAY FIVE - PLAN

BREAKFAST
Meditation OR Dry Skin Brushing before shower and
Fruit salad OR Smoothie, 1 cup preferred juice, 1 cup
water, 1 tbsp Rice Bran or chia seeds or LSA

Juice option– Beetroot/ Watermelon/ Berries

LUNCH
Fresh salad or steamed vegetables, lemon juice, olive
oil and herbs/spices as dressing OR Soup
Feel free to add beans or Tuna/Salmon, Brown rice or
quinoa, nuts seeds

DINNER
Steamed or roasted mixed veggies with herbs and
spices (veggie curry/ casserole) - Can include beans
and lentils, brown rice

Can re-introduce organic chicken or Egg

SNACKS (OPTIONAL)
Celery, capsicum or cucumber sticks or nuts if needed
Carrot sticks with homemade hummus or tahini dip -
Piece of fruit

Protein ball – 100g coconut, 100g Almonds, 100g
Cashews, tsp cinnamon, tsp cacao, blended with 2 tbs
coconut oil, 6 medjool dates, 1 tsp vanilla, 20 g dried
cranberries – makes 12 if you roll them into balls, can
also be good over fruit salad or in smoothie for breakfast

BEFORE BED
1 cup apple or prune juice, 1 cup water, 1 tbsp Rice
Bran/LSA – ideally blended together

WATER
2 litres throughout the day

EXERCISE
20 min walk OR Yoga

JOURNAL

DAY SIX – ACTIONS

Today's Intention: I am letting go

Action Step: Declutter your inbox

Now that you're body is letting go of clutter, it's time to start clearing the clutter of your external life. How's your inbox looking? An overflowing inbox can drain your energy. Emails should have 3 options when they reach your inbox; they are either immediate, need to be filed in their subject or are for the trash straight away. Once sorted, aim to check email at specific times during the day instead of feeling you have to reply to every email the second it arrives. This can drain energy due to the ongoing stress of trying to keep on top of it.

CLEAN EATING

Water- 2 Litres a day

CHILL PILL

Gratitude

In your journal tonight, focus on what you are grateful for today. The break you took in the sun for 5 minutes, the chat you had with your mum on the phone, the amazing presentation you gave. List everything no matter how big or small and flood your cells with new and positive feelings.

Then start to explore what gives you energy in life. Do the people or situations in your life make you feel tired or inspired? Schedule one of the things or people that make you feel inspired for next weekend.

DAY SIX - PLAN

BREAKFAST
Meditation OR Dry skin brushing before shower and
Fruit Salad – Smoothie - 1 cup preferred juice, 1 cup
water, 1 tbsp Rice Bran OR chia seeds OR LSA

Cup of bone broth or stock

Juice option - Cucumber, celery, mint, lime and kiwi fruit

LUNCH
Fresh salad, roasted or steamed vegetables, lemon
juice, olive oil and herbs/spices as dressing OR Soup
Can add beans or tuna if you like

DINNER
Steamed mixed veggies with herbs and spices (veg
curry/ casserole) - Can include beans and lentils
Can include grain-fed beef or organic chicken or egg

SNACKS (OPTIONAL)
Celery or cucumber sticks or nuts if needed
Carrot sticks with homemade hummus or tahini dip –
Protein ball, piece of fruit

BEFORE BED
1 cup apple or prune juice, 1 cup water, 1 tbsp Rice
Bran/LSA

WATER
2 litres throughout the day

EXERCISE
20 min walk OR yoga or Meditation

GRATITUDE JOURNAL

DAY SEVEN - ACTIONS

Today's Intention: I love and accept myself exactly as I am, right now.

Get Grounded

We spend so much time in our head - over analysing, over thinking that it can make us anxious, stressed and overwhelmed. The best way to 'ground' our energy is to sit with your bare feet on grass. There is some amazing research about this called 'Earthing.'

CLEAN EATING

Good fats/Bad fats: Guess what... Not all fat makes you fat!! Hooray - this is the best news ever. In fact good fats can help you to detox and also in fact lose weight! Double Hoorah!! Like I mentioned earlier fats make up 80% of your brain - so they are in fact a 'must eat' item. So how do you know which the goodies are and which are the baddies?

Good fats are found in:

Nuts (walnuts, almonds, brazils, cashews, pecans, macadamias), Avocado, Coconut Oil, Wild Caught Salmon, Chia Seeds, Hemp Seeds, Grass-Fed Butter.

Bad fats are found in:

Trans fats are the baddies and the main culprits are margarine, vegetable oil and any product made using these - think fried food, packaged food, biscuits, crackers, doughnuts, pies and cakes.

CHILL PILL

CHILL PILL

Bath with Epsom Salts and Aromatherapy

A great way to help toxins gently leave the body is with an Epsom salt bath. A handful of Epsom salts in your bath water will create a gradient for toxins to release from your skin - the body's largest organ of elimination, which has been working overtime to support you during your detox. This is particularly effective at releasing lactic acid built up in tense muscles. Add a few drops of a relaxing essential oil such as Lavender or Chamomile and you are priming your body to let go deeply for a healing night of restful sleep.

DAY SEVEN - PLAN

BREAKFAST
Meditation or Dry skin brushing before shower and Fruit
Salad – Smoothie - 1 cup preferred juice, 1 cup water, 1
tbsp Rice Bran OR chia seeds OR LSA

Juice option- Pear, Apple, Carrot, Cucumber, Ginger

LUNCH
Fresh salad or steamed vegetables, lemon juice, olive
oil and herbs/spices as dressing – OR Soup
Brown rice, quinoa, tuna or beans can be added

DINNER
Steamed or roasted mixed veggies with herbs and
spices (veggie curry/casserole) - Can include beans,
lentils, brown rice, fish, salmon, grain fed beef, organic
chicken

SNACKS (OPTIONAL)
Celery or cucumber sticks or nuts if needed
Carrot sticks with homemade hummus or tahini dip –
Protein balls or bone broth or Piece of fruit

BEFORE BED
1 cup apple or prune juice, 1 cup water, 1 tbsp Rice
Bran/LSA

WATER
2 litres throughout the day

EXERCISE

20 min walk OR Yoga OR Meditation

GRATITUDE JOURNAL or Epsom salt bath

RECIPES AND JUICING

BENEFITS OF COMMONLY JUICED FRUITS AND VEGGIES

Apples: High in antioxidants and detoxifiers. Sweetens bitter juice. Aids in digestion.

Kale: Amazing for the blood and skin. Rich in dozens of vitamins and minerals. Has major anti-oxidant activity.

Lemons: Super alkalizing. Makes any juice easy to drink and deliciously tart.

Carrots: Also high in antioxidants and other vitamins and minerals including folic acid and B vitamins. Adds a slight sweetness to juices.

Cucumbers: Great for skin and hair. High water content is perfect for hydration. Aids in weight loss.

Ginger: Amazing for digestive upset. Helps with allergies, colds and coughs. Anti-inflammatory.

Cilantro: Incredibly good for detoxifying the body. Helps chelate heavy metals out of the body. Anti-inflammatory. Great for hormone balancing.

Parsley: Another major detoxifier. Improves body odor and breath. High in chlorophyll which oxidizes the blood. Helps the body hold onto iron.

Beetroot: Blood purifier and blood builder. Prevents and helps dissolve stones in liver, kidneys and bladder.

TIPS AND TRICKS

If you plan on juicing a lot, buy in bulk. I usually buy a 2kg bag of carrots and oranges at a time and big bags of apples and lemons. See what is available in your area because it's much cheaper to shop this way.

Clean straight away. Your juicer is really easy to clean if you do it right after juicing. If you have a 'Ninja' or bullet, even easier. I usually rinse everything off before I devour my juice. If you let it sit for a while, it will take a bit more effort to get everything clean and it just takes more time.

Use more veggies than fruit. One common mistake is to juice mostly fruits to make your juices sweet. You can easily overload on sugar if you're not careful. You will see that 1 apple or a lemon goes a long way in juice and carrots are surprisingly sweet. Try to use more cucumbers, greens, and celery.

Only drink 200ml at a time. It's easy to over drink juices because they're just so good and good for you. Your body can only process 200ml every hour, so any more than that is a waste

RESOURCES AND MOTIVATION

Being motivated is a key part of staying on track and being inspired for the full seven days. Lack of support and motivation is one of the biggest reasons people don't follow through.

Below I have some of my favourite documentaries and books to keep you motivated and expand what you know about your own health and wellbeing.

Documentaries:

That Sugar Film (2014)

Hungry for Change (2012)

Fat, Sick and Nearly Dead (2010)

Food Matters (2008)

Food Inc (2008)

You Can Heal Your Life (2007)

Books:

Crazy, Sexy Diet – Kris Carr

The Real Food Chef – Dr Libby Weaver

FedUp – Sue Dengate

I Quit Sugar – Sarah Wilson

Family Food – Pete Evans

About the Author

Tammy Guest
Naturopath | Coach | Speaker | Entrepreneur

Tammy Guest is a degree-qualified naturopath with a medical science background. Practicing for over eight years, Tammy has helped thousands of clients take control of their health through a whole life approach, which has seen them be less stressed, have more energy and live a life they love.

With a focus on adrenal fatigue in entrepreneurs and business people Tammy loves creating opportunities for change on a cellular level through her Inspirational Health Clinic.

When she's not bushwalking with her family, she's learning to fly helicopters, writing her book or running retreats in Asia and Australia.

You can find out more
www.tammyguest.com
https://www.instagram.com/tammyguests/
https://www.facebook.com/tammyguesthealth/
https://au.linkedin.com/in/inspirationaltammyguest

www.ingramcontent.com/pod-product-compliance
Lightning Source LLC
Chambersburg PA
CBHW060039030426

42334CB00019B/2396